Cherished

The kinds of things every girl needs to know are in this book. It's completely awesome – it totally made me think. I'm going to recommend it to all my friends.
Jayne Drury, teenage girl

Cherished is such a beautiful, heart-touching, thought provoking, challenging and inspiring book. It covers so many issues that us girls go through whilst being refined in to the 'golden girl' that God created us to be. This is the modern girls' must-have manual to taking those vital steps (in well heeled shoes!) to blossoming as a 'lady of the Lord'. Buy two. One for you and one for a friend!
Gemma Hunt, TV Presenter

Rachel has a fantastic ability to go where many fear to tread, tackling the big issues head on with honesty, insight and humour. This book packs a powerful message, helping girls to understand their real value and see who God has created them to be. It's a fantastic resource.
Mike Pilavachi, Soul Survivor

Rachel's done a great job combining humour, reflection, challenges and facts to explore what it means TODAY to become a girl of God. It is well written and accessible to the individual, or could form the basis for a group study and reflection. I highly recommend it.
Revd. Tim Sudworth, Co-author of Mission-Shaped Youth

Cherished is essential reading for every girl navigating the exciting, but challenging, teenage years. It's honest about the real issues and yet it's thoroughly practical. As you read the pages that follow you'll feel like your best friend is writing to you – longing for you to be all that God intended you to be. Why settle for less?
Matt Summerfield, Urban Saints

Cherished

Boys, bodies and becoming a girl of gold

Rachel Gardner

Foreword by Ali Martin of Soul Sista

INTER-VARSITY PRESS
Norton Street, Nottingham NG7 3HR, England
Email: ivp@ivpbooks.com
Website: www.ivpbooks.com

First published 2009
Reprinted 2009, 2010

British Library Cataloguing in Publication Data
A catalogue record for this book is available from the British Library.

ISBN: 978-1-84474-389-6

Set in 10/12pt Myriad
Typeset in Great Britain by CRB Associates, Potterhanworth, Lincolnshire
Printed and bound in Great Britain by Ashford Colour Press Ltd, Gosport, Hampshire

Inter-Varsity Press publishes Christian books that are true to the Bible and that communicate the gospel, develop discipleship and strengthen the church for its mission in the world.

Inter-Varsity Press is closely linked with the Universities and Colleges Christian Fellowship, a student movement connecting Christian Unions in universities and colleges throughout Great Britain, and a member movement of the International Fellowship of Evangelical Students.
Website: *www.uccf.org.uk*

For Mercy, Cosi, Zola, Hephzibah, Tirzah, Maddie,
Victoria and Sienna

May you always shine brightly like stars in the night sky

For Timothy and Jonathan

May the girl of your dreams know that you will help her chase hers

Acknowledgments
To a few lovely folk

A few years ago a small team of us began the journey of the Romance Academy. I am so grateful to Jason, Dan, Gordon, Rachael and Ian for their vision and commitment from the very beginning. I also want to thank all the young people and youth workers who have been part of our story and continue to paint a new and hope-filled future for other young people.

Thank you to my supportive family for rooting me in love and *Pride and Prejudice*.

Where would any of us be without our wise and crazy friends? Thank you to all my girly mates, from whom I have gleaned priceless wisdom and embarrassing stories!

Thank you to Kate and the IVP team for their insight and encouragement.

Jason, you are my heart's companion, and I cherish every day spent with you.

'Cherish'

[from Middle English *cherishen*, from Old French *cherir*, *cheriss*, *cher*, from Latin *carus*]
  • to protect and treat with great care and affection/to treasure/
    to nurture/to think well of

Contents

Foreword

Reading *Cherished* is like having a good natter with a fun and very wise best friend, someone who tells it like it is, cheers you on, points you towards God and has a good giggle along the way. If you're looking to understand yourself, God and the world around you better, *Cherished* is for you. If you want to know more about the God who loves you, this book is a must.

Cherished is full of real advice and practical wisdom, packed full of great stories, and constantly drawing from the Word of God and the experience of others to help steer us through the complicated path of changing bodies, raging hormones, crazy crushes and setting good sexual boundaries. It is an interesting and gripping read though it goes way beyond that, giving opportunities to pause and reflect, to take the truth and apply it to our own lives, and to stop and think about what we've read. *Cherished* becomes a companion for engaging with God and the big issues of life, cheering us on to becoming a girl of gold.

I can honestly say that Rachel herself is a particularly awesome girl of gold. In the time I've been privileged to know her and hang out with her I've loved seeing her love for God and others affect everything she says and does, making me laugh one minute and cry the next! She is full of wisdom, grace and fun – and all this overflows into her amazing book.

I really encourage you to pick up *Cherished* and have a read. As you do you will hear the voice of a woman who truly wants the best for you, who truly wants you to succeed in life, and who truly wants you to understand yourself better and point you towards God. You will also hear the voice of that same God telling you over and again how much he loves you, cares for you, and has great plans for you. The truth of *Cherished* has the potential to change the rest of your life. Read it, love it, live it and go for it!

Ali Martin, Soul Sista

Introduction: Cherished

I have written this book for you.

I realize that you probably don't know me and I don't know you, so it might feel a bit weird my saying that, but it's true! I have written this book because I want to let you in on a bit of a secret.

You are precious, and your life is a gift to you.

It's a secret because few of us know it and even fewer actually believe it.

The best thing about it is that your preciousness has nothing to do with you. Sound strange? Read on.

Imagine you were told by a reliable source that there was a box of diamonds buried under the local skate park. Imagine that, late one night, you manage to persuade your friends to sneak into the park and dig through the concrete! It's back-breaking work. After a while one of your friends shouts, 'I've found something!' and you all crowd round. As the dust settles you see a box in your friend's hands. She takes the lid off and you look inside. Can you imagine how you feel when you realize that inside the box is just a lump of black rock? Is that it? You were expecting glittering diamonds. You were picturing a life of wealth and luxury. How gutted would you feel?

A week later you get a text from your 'reliable source'. It reads, 'Any luck finding the diamonds?' Feeling a bit miffed, you chuck the lump of rock into your bag and take the short bus ride to meet your 'source'. 'It's nothing, just an old rock!' you say when you arrive. 'I can't believe I spent the night digging up the skate park floor for this. You can keep it!' Your source picks up the bag and takes out the rock. Then she puts on a pair of very odd-looking glasses. Holding the rock very close to her eyes, she is silent for a while and then says, 'Um, just what I thought; priceless. This diamond is totally unique.'

Hidden in the lump of coal is a priceless diamond. You looked and saw a rock; the 'source' (who is in fact a top jeweller) looked and saw a priceless diamond. Even though everyone else overlooked it, she knew what they were missing because she knew what she was looking for.

That's the thing about true value – it never changes. It just sometimes gets missed if people don't know what they are looking for.

Do you feel valued, treasured, cherished?

I hope that you have people in your life who look at you and see how precious you are. It might be your mum or gran, your dad, your teacher or a close friend. Even though your relationship with them isn't always perfect, you know deep down that they love you.

I have written this book for you, because when God looks at you he knows what he is looking for – and he sees how precious you are.

Or you might be struggling to think of people in your life who treat you well. They might say they love you or are there for you, but they are unkind to you and regularly let you down.

As you read this book I hope you will see how you can treasure yourself and your relationships with friends and family.

I hope you will feel inspired to discover ways of exploring your abilities and dreams.

I hope you will be encouraged to protect your heart and still keep it open to God and others.

I hope you will appreciate your life and the mysteries in the world around you.

But none of this happens overnight. It takes time to grow into the woman you dream of becoming.

Wonder_land

How good are you at stopping and thinking?
Pretty good? Not bad? Rubbish?

Do you sometimes find yourself caught between dreaming about tomorrow and living in the past? How often do you think about what you are going through right now? Do you know how you are feeling and why? Sometimes our thoughts and emotions are all a bit too confusing to deal with. It can be hard to work out who we are in a world that constantly tells us that we need to be pretty, thin, popular and sexy.

One of the best ways to get to know more about yourself is to spend time with yourself! At the end of each chapter, there are a couple of ideas to help

you get to know yourself better. 'Wonder_land' is a collection of questions for you to think over and challenge yourself with. You could do it alone or grab some friends you trust to think through the questions with you.

My Sanctuary

But knowing more about yourself is not just about you! It's also about listening to your Creator and getting his perspective on your life. 'My Sanctuary' is a chance for you to find a still and safe place where you can stop and listen. God wants you to listen to what he thinks and feels about you.

In your sanctuary you can be you, just you, with God.

I really want to encourage you to take time to find your sanctuary. Here are some questions to ask yourself to help you find your still and safe space:

- Am I free to think for myself here?
- Will this place help me to remember things that have happened in my life so far?
- Will I be able to dream about my future here?
- Can I discover treasure about myself here?
- Is it comfortable?
- Do I feel safe here?

Your sanctuary could be anywhere: your bedroom, the loo, a local coffee shop, the corner of a garden or park, a room at school or the youth centre.

It might even be a person you know will listen to you and help you think through things. To help you choose who to talk to you could ask the same questions as before:

- Do they help me to think for myself?
- Will they help me to remember things that have happened in my life so far?
- Will they help me dream for my future?
- Can they help me discover treasure about myself?
- Are they comfortable to be with?
- Do I feel safe being with them?

Sanctuaries can also be holy places. I believe that what makes your sanctuary holy and safe is the fact that God is with you wherever you are. His presence changes everything. He longs to help you live your life with hope and confidence. Finding a sanctuary will help to remind you that God always wants to speak to you, wherever you are and whatever you are doing.

A number of brilliant girls have helped me to write this book. I hope that their stories will help you discover more about yourself and how precious you are. They have discovered that it's really important to be honest about the painful stuff in life and to get excited about the future and all the possibilities that face us. Whoever you are and wherever you have come from, God's gift of life is for you and he wants to help you to live it. He made you to live your life to the full, not sitting on the edge waiting for it to begin or blaming other people for who you are and where you have got to.

Who knows what your future holds?

Who knows where your life will lead?

Here's a prayer my friend Laura wrote:

> *Lord, please help me to find myself.*
> *Please help me to find reasons and possibilities that can be*
> *life-changing.*
> *Please be with me on the journey to finding life and more about the*
> *wonders of this beautiful world. Amen.*

(Used by permission)

There are so many exciting mysteries and adventures before you. As daunting as life can seem, we can depend fully on God our Father to be with us from here into the future. Even in the dark times, when we feel lost and alone, we can reach out to our Creator and Friend and know that his love will always surround us.

> *God's watching every step you take,*
> *Sorting out shade for your unprotected side . . .*
> *God'll protect you, won't let harm near you;*
> *He'll keep his eye on you, check you're OK.*
> *God's tuned into your life, as you stay in or hit the town,*
> *Right now and every single day.*

(Psalm 121:1–8)

So, whatever you choose to do with your life, I hope that you cherish it as a gift from God to you.

The way you live your life is your way of honouring him and the way he has created and is creating you. So whether God is fully in the picture for you right now or not, may these words of wisdom pour into your life the kind of things that help you know that you are lovely, lovable, unique, full of potential and, above all, cherished.

Rachel x

Chapter One
The Beginning of Mysteries

The crime scene was eerie and quiet. There was evidence in the room of a fight; chairs had been knocked over and a picture lay smashed on the floor. The murderer had obviously made a speedy exit through the large window that was wide open, and there were muddy footprints all round the dead body. I thought for a while, mulling over all the evidence that lay before me, trying to solve the mystery. People around were all looking at me, waiting for my answer. Eventually it came to me. It was so obvious; why had I taken so long to work it out?

'Bart Simpson did it!' I said. 'He killed Mo in the Kwick-e-mart with a doughnut!'

OK, so winning at Simpsons Cluedo® doesn't make me a top murder detective. But I can't help being fascinated by a good mystery that needs solving.

What's the biggest puzzle you've ever solved?

What's the greatest mystery you have ever come across?

You don't need to look too far to find one. The truth is that *you* are one of the greatest mysteries the universe has to offer.

Do you ever think about yourself like that – a mystery?

You are a mystery because there is so much that you don't know about yourself yet. It's true for every single human being on the planet. The journey of life takes us to places and through experiences that teach us loads about ourselves and our world. Sometimes we like what we see. Other times we feel ashamed about how we or others behave, and commit ourselves to putting things right.

The mystery of being alive makes us ask loads of questions. Why are we here? What is life all about? Is there anyone who can guide us through this mysterious and confusing life? How can we get the most out of this life? What happens if things go wrong?

When you were little, you weren't asking these questions. You were too busy playing with friends, working out what kind of ice cream you liked or how to do your hair, or discovering ways to thump your brother without getting caught!

When you became a teenager, a whole new set of things became important. The big question that you and every other young person are asking yourselves is 'Who am I?' It sounds easy enough to answer, doesn't it? 'My name is Rachel; I live in North London, I love dogs and hate rice pudding' . . . but it's way more complex than that. You are discovering things about your emotions, your abilities, your likes and dislikes and what you believe are the right and wrong things to do. Every day you compare yourself with others. Every day things happen that get you thinking about what you believe is true. You might even start making plans in your head about who you want to be in the future.

All this is shaping your character and personality. It's making you you! And it can feel overwhelming. You are still you, but you are also changing. There are some days when you act like a kid and other days when you act like an adult – it's confusing to your parents, your teachers and your friends, and to you!

We live in a world that sends us loads of messages about what we should be doing, wearing, eating, buying and watching. There's no way that we can do or have everything the world offers us, and trying to get it all will just leave us exhausted and unfulfilled. We need to make choices all the time about what we will and what we won't strive after. We make choices like these every day – sometimes without even realizing it.

Some people think that the only things really worth striving for are money, beauty and fame. They pour everything they have and own into being stupidly rich, breathtakingly beautiful or ridiculously famous. But the sad truth is that none of these things have what it takes to help us live our lives to the fullest and best. Why? Because, no matter how much we have, we will always want more – we will never be satisfied.

The God who made us asks that we put all of our heart and soul into getting to know him.

The Bible calls this 'wisdom'.

Information lets you know what might happen if you make certain choices; wisdom helps you know whether you are living the best kind of life. For example, information might tell you that the guy in the local newsagents never asks young people for ID when they buy cigarettes, so you can buy them without getting into trouble. Wisdom tells you that, whether he asks for ID or not, smoking is going to mess up your health and will not help you live your life to the full. Wisdom is about using your experience and knowledge and advice from people you trust to help you choose the best in life. God's wisdom brings us peace, joy and total satisfaction in life.

Do you want this? Then listen to these words, written thousands of years ago:

> *My daughter, listen to me and treasure my instructions.*
> *Tune your ears to wisdom and concentrate on understanding.*
> *Cry out for insight and understanding.*
> *Search for them as you would for lost money or hidden treasure . . .*
> *Then you will understand what is right, just, and fair, and you will*
> *know how to choose the right thing to do every time.*
> *For wisdom will enter your heart,*
> *And knowledge will fill you with joy.*
> *Wise planning will watch over you*
> *And understanding will keep you safe.*
>
> (Proverbs 2:1–4, 9–11)

What are you crying out for? What are you striving after? Would you rather be famous or happy? Would you rather be searching for wealth or for wisdom?

Being wise isn't about being clever, religious or old! It's about realizing more and more each day how much we need the help of God, mates and family to live lives that we can be proud of and fulfilled in. Really wise young women know that the best people to listen to are those who can help them live life to the full. You know that they have good things to say because of the way they treat themselves and other people. What they tell you is way more than simply information about what to do and what not to do. They help you discover the best way to live.

In a scene from the US TV series *One Tree Hill*[1], one character, Hailey, says:

> *The rest of your life is a long time. And whether you know it or not, it is being shaped right now. You can choose to blame your circumstances and bad luck or bad choices or you can fight back. Things aren't always going to be fair in the real world – that's just the way it is. But for the most part you get what you give . . . The rest of your life is being shaped right now by the dreams you chase, the choices you make, and the person you decide to be. The rest of your life is a long time and it starts right now.*

There will be times when you will be challenged by what you read in this book, and that's good! I think it is very important for you to know who you are and why you feel and think as you do. You are unique and precious. Your thoughts, feelings and dreams matter. When you feel challenged, stop and think. It's OK to ask questions, and it's OK to change your mind.

Wonder_land

Here are some questions for you to have a think about. You could even try these out on your friends.

- Look back over the year since your last birthday: what has changed for you? (E.g. your hair is longer or shorter, you have moved house, changed school etc . . .) What have you changed your mind about recently?

- What things concern you at the moment?
- What are your dreams for your future?
- What are your parent's or carer's dreams for your future? Could you ask them? I wonder if some of them are the same as yours?
- What do you think God's dreams for your future are?
- If you like writing, why not write a letter to the future you? You could share your hopes and concerns with yourself. You could even seal it in an envelope and store it somewhere safe, to be opened at a much later date!

My Sanctuary

Have you found your sanctuary space? Good. Now, take a few deep breaths and feel yourself slowing down and calming down. Ninety-five per cent of our energy comes from breathing, but the problem is that most of us breathe too quickly and not deeply enough, so we don't get the full benefit of a good gulp of fresh air!

So why not breathe in deeply. Hold it. Then breathe out.

Try this a few times. (You might feel a bit light-headed. This is because your body and brain are not used to getting this much oxygen at one go.)

As you slow down your breathing and prepare to listen to God, choose one word to say slowly in your head, over and over again. It could be any word that will help you focus on being still and open to God (cherished, loved, Jesus, or open . . .). When your thoughts keep wandering all over the place, use this word to bring yourself back to focusing on listening to God.

After you have done this a few times, try out the following activity.

This line represents the story of your life. Grab a pen and fill in your date of birth by the trainers over on the left and today's date by the ankle boots near to the other end of the line. By the remaining pairs of shoes, write down any events or memories of your life that are important or significant to you.

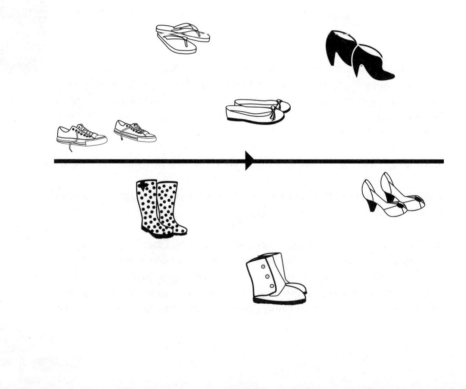

Once you have filled in all that you want to, sit back and take a look at your timeline. How do you feel about the journey of your life so far? The Bible says that God is always with you; he never falls asleep or forgets about you. Close your eyes and picture God with you in every moment of your life. Can you feel his presence with you now?

In this safe and still place, speak to God. Share your thoughts with him. Then stop, and listen.

He wants to speak to you too.

> *Draw close to God and God will draw close to you.*   (James 4:8)

Chapter Two
Lovely Label

There was one day at school each year that I hated.

We called it 'mufti day' – it meant that you could ditch school uniform and wear whatever you wanted. My friends spent ages planning what to wear; I spent ages working out ways to make my mum think that I was too ill to go to school because I had nothing fashionable to wear. My parents were both out of work so we had no spare money for new clothes. Most of the time this didn't bother me, but on 'mufti day' it became all too clear that I didn't fit in.

I remember persuading a friend one 'mufti day' to lend me some of her clothes. She was slimmer and shorter than me and I spent the whole day bulging out of an outfit that was way too small! I drew attention to myself by looking so uncomfortable. I desperately wanted to look like my friends and be accepted by them. I ended up feeling like I had a huge label across my forehead saying that I was a loser and boring.

There is nothing wrong with wanting to fit in. Everyone feels like this from time to time. The problem starts when fitting in with everyone else becomes the only way we can like ourselves and find out who we are. When we don't know who we are, we are quicker to accept other people's ideas about ourselves. This can sometimes get us into difficult situations.

Ellie hadn't meant to steal the pair of shoes from River Island, but Mounisha was so persuasive.

'Stop worrying about it; you won't get caught. People do it all the time. I'll give you a tenner if you do it.'

So she did, and she got caught by the store security guard. As she was led away to a room at the back of the shop to wait for the police, Ellie saw Mounisha run away without even looking back.

Thinking that friends will like you *only* if you do what they want to or if you dress just like them will always end in loneliness. If you always go with the flow even when your conscience tells you it's wrong, then you won't be giving people the chance to get to know and like the real you. You could even end up disliking yourself.

At the beginning of the film *Jane Eyre*[1] (which is based on a brilliant book[2]), we see a very young Jane being mistreated by her aunt and cousins, with whom she lives. They treat her so badly that in the end she begins to fight back. Her aunt packs her off to a boarding school for very poor girls and on her first day she is made to stand on a stool with the word 'LIAR' on a label round her neck. The rest of the school are banned from talking to her for a week as her punishment for being a liar.

But the fact is that Jane is not a liar, and only one girl sees this: a redhaired girl called Helen, who later becomes Jane's greatest friend. Their friendship changes Jane's life. Had she not met Helen, she might have believed for the rest of her life that she was worthless and unlovable. Helen's love for her gives her a new way of seeing herself.

What's Your Name?

If you could choose to be called by a different name for a whole day, what would it be?

And how would it make you see yourself?

How would your name make you act?

For the last couple of years I have helped to lead a youth club at our church. I love sitting at the hair and nail bar chatting to the girls (and some of the guys who want black or pink nails!) about what's going on in their world. I find out who is going out with who and who said what about whose brother . . . you know the kind of thing!

A while ago I started getting to know a bunch of girls who called themselves 'hos', 'sluts' and 'bitches'. I hate those words, so you can imagine how I reacted when the girls told me. I said things like, 'What? Who calls you that? Don't listen to them. Stand up for yourself!' and things like that.

When I had calmed down, one of the girls asked me, 'What's the matter, Rachel? It's just what we say to each other. It doesn't mean anything.'

It doesn't mean anything – really?

I don't agree.

The nicknames we get called or call ourselves are very powerful. They can give us an identity and are like labels that stick to us and begin to influence how we feel and behave. If people tell you that you are stupid for long enough, you will begin to believe them, even though it's not true. You might even start acting a bit stupid, because that's all people expect of you.

I know a girl whose dad keeps telling her that she is an accident, a mistake, a waste of space. Another girl I work with is constantly being told by her mum that she won't amount to much, that she needs to be more like her sister, that all she is good at is running away when the going gets tough.

All these 'names' are lies. They are not what God says about you.

Even if your parents tell you they didn't want you, even if you are regularly compared with your sister, even if your so-called friends spread untrue rumours about you, the truth about your real identity and value is so amazing. It's amazing because it's true, and it's true because it's what God says.

God says that he knows you and loves you (1 John 4:9).

God says that you belong to him as his daughter (1 John 4:4).

God says that he knows your potential and is excited about your life (Jeremiah 29:11).

A girl who knows she is 'covered' in labels telling her how much she is loved and how precious she is has no spare space for labels with names like 'disappointment', 'loser' or 'waste of space'.

The names that belong to you are: 'lovely', 'cherished', 'unique', 'loved', 'precious', 'beautiful', 'lovable', 'creative'.

This is because you have been created by a God who has made you like this. God covers us all with these labels. This is our identity.

But it doesn't stop here. God has also made us all unique, with different characters and qualities. You are going to have some identity traits that not everyone else has: these may include 'adventurous', 'compassionate', 'fearless', 'strong', 'gentle', 'peaceful', 'passionate', 'resourceful.'

Coke-can Confidence

A while ago, I did an experiment with a group of young people. I asked for two volunteers to have a go at crushing a Coke can with their bare hands. I chose one lad who looked really strong, and a smaller girl. I handed them both a can and asked them to squeeze it as hard as they could.

The lad concentrated all his effort into squashing the can, but with no success.

The girl managed to crush her can in one easy squeeze!

How did this happen? To all the young people watching the experiment, it seemed obvious that the lad should have won the competition. But he didn't; the girl won.

You may have guessed how she managed to do this.

The night before, I had pierced a hole in the bottom of one of the cans and drained all the Coke out of it. I handed the lad the can that was still full of Coke and gave the girl the can that looked full but was in fact empty. When she put even the smallest amount of pressure on it, it crumpled.

Knowing that we belong to God is like being a can full of Coca-Cola®. No matter how much pressure is put on you, you don't crumple.

As well as pouring his love into your heart, God has given you skills and talents that can help you grow in confidence. It could be anything: singing, making people laugh, cooking, writing poetry, sport, playing computer games, designing outfits, caring for people in your family. Have you noticed that when you spend time doing what you love, you feel better about yourself and happier with other people? It gives you confidence because it makes you feel stronger inside and gives you a feeling of purpose.

Paul, one of the first Christians to teach about Jesus, told the new Christians that God had given all of them different skills and gifts:

> God has given each of us the ability to do certain things well. So if God has given you the gift of prophecy, speak out when you have faith that God is speaking through you. If your gift is that of serving others, serve them well. If you are a teacher, do a good job of teaching. If your job is to encourage others, do it! If you have money, share it generously. If God has given you leadership ability, take the responsibility seriously. And if you have the gift of showing kindness, do it gladly.
>
> (Romans 12:6–8)

All of us have skills and talents given to us by God, and we need to use them. As you grow older it is important to know the skills and abilities God has given you. This will help you to understand God's will for your life and to live it to the full.

Good relationships with people can help us grow in confidence too. Children who are supported and encouraged to try new things are often more confident than children who have no support or interest from parents or carers.

But sometimes we can have a crisis in confidence even with something we are good at.

If you are good at singing, it can be hard to handle if a girl comes along who is better than you. Some pretty girls struggle when there are other pretty girls around. If you are the one who always gets the highest mark in maths, you can feel devastated if your results come back a bit lower than you (and your parents) expected.

Your abilities and talents are not dependent on your winning all the time. Healthy competition is good, but needing always to be the best can make you feel unhappy or insecure around people. Sometimes I think that girls are the worst at this kind of competitiveness. Rather than seeing other girls as a threat, we need to be confident in our abilities and skills and be pleased for other girls when they do well at something. There is nothing more unattractive than jealousy. There is nothing more beautiful than being able to appreciate your own abilities and other people's skills.

It all comes back to knowing that God made and loves us, and letting that give us our identity. Look at these words written thousands of years ago about how precious and well designed you are:

You created every part of me;
you put me together in my mother's womb . . .
When my bones were being formed,
carefully put together in my mother's womb.
When I was growing in secret,
you knew that I was there – you saw me before I was born.
The days allotted to me have all been recorded in your book,
before any of them ever began.

(Psalm 139)

God has created you in a unique and amazing way. He made you to be just you, which means that there will be times when you think, feel or look differently from other people, and that's good! This will help you encourage others to be themselves too. God made everyone in a way that is uniquely precious to him – so you don't need to fall into the habit of being overly critical about yourself and judgmental of others.

Right here and now you can start trying out being who *you* are. The rest of your life starts now, so don't grow up pretending to be someone else or hiding who you are. There is so much pressure on you to be like others. Now is your time to explore being who God made you.

Paul prayed this prayer for his friends over a thousand years ago. This is also my prayer for you:

I pray that from God's glorious, unlimited resources he will give you mighty inner strength through his Holy Spirit. And I pray that Jesus will be more and more at home in your hearts as you trust in him. May your roots go down deep into the soil of God's marvellous love. And may you have power to understand, as all God's people should, how long, how high, and how deep his love really is. May you experience the love of Christ, though it is so great you will never fully understand it. Then you will be filled with the fullness of life and power that comes from God.

(Ephesians 3:16–19)

Paul was so convinced of the power of Jesus' love that he knew that if his friends were to really experience it, their lives would be changed for ever.

The greatest truth about your identity you will ever discover is that you are loved by God.

Wonder_land

- How far have you been prepared to go to fit in with others? Or how far have you gone to get noticed?
- Who do you most want to be accepted by?
- Have you ever been labelled with a lie? How has this made you feel? How has this made you act?
- Have you ever been tempted to begin to believe the lie?
- Be honest now: have you ever labelled someone else with a lie? Why did you do this? Do you know how it affected the person? Are you able to do anything about it?
- What are some of the things you do that give you confidence? Is there anything new you would like to try to build your confidence, such as take up a sport or a hobby with friends?

- Do you have a close friend you can be yourself with, or a parent/youth leader/teacher who will help you work out your talents and strengths?

It can be really hard to be honest with ourselves about what we are good at and what really isn't our 'thing'. This is your chance to reflect on who you are: your strengths and weaknesses. There is no-one on the whole planet who has only weaknesses, so as you begin this reflection don't write yourself off. God has created you in awesome and unique ways, and he is proud of you. Knowing more about how he has made us can help us feel happier with who we are, and less likely to feel threatened by other people.

As you start out, take a few deep breaths and invite God to help you find out more about how he has made you. He may want to help you to grow stronger in some things. He may want to help you work on some of the areas you struggle with.

My Character

Look at this list of characteristics and circle in one colour any words that you feel describe positive aspects of your character:

kind / controlling / creative / adventurous / aggressive / cheerful /

spontaneous / cynical / patient / brave / honest / loyal /

supportive / bossy / faithful / fearful / compassionate /

gentle / strong / self-centred / fun

Take another colour and circle words that describe the more negative aspects of your character.

Look back over the words you have circled. How do you feel about these words? Do you feel brave enough to show them to a friend who knows you well to see if they would agree with your picture of yourself?

Now choose one word that you have circled in each colour. Write them in the block below:

I have been thinking about who I am. I reckon that one of my great strengths is that I am

_____

_____

I am so glad that this is one of my strengths. I notice that it makes people around me feel

_____

_____

I will enjoy continuing to grow in this strength. It's my way of glorifying God in my life.

I reckon that one of my weaknesses is that I can be

_____

_____

I am glad that I am able to be honest about this. I know that there are times when acting like this makes people around me feel

_____

_____

I will continue to be honest about this aspect of my character and find a wise woman to help me work at it. It's my way of glorifying God in my life.

My Talents

One of the best ways to think about where your talents lie is to make a list of all the things you enjoy doing or being involved in:

1. _____

2. _____

3. _____

4. _____

5. _____

Look at the list you have made – it doesn't matter how many things you have written down. Use your pen to put a tick next to the activity that:

- you really enjoy getting involved in
- makes you feel happier with yourself when you do it
- people you trust say you are good at

- you work hard at getting better at (you practise regularly or spend your free time doing it).

Look back over your list. Thank God for the skills and talents he has given you. Why not show someone your list and ask them to help you find out more about the way God has made you and wants to work through you?

My Sanctuary

Even If you know what you are good at and enjoy doing, the smallest lie or unkind comment can still sometimes really knock your confidence.

Take a few moments to write on your label a lie that someone has told about you that you believed or still believe. It could be something like:

- You are no good at school.
- You are a waste of space.
- You are boring.
- You . . .

_____

_____

Write it down in the space above.

Think for a moment why it is that this lie still has power to make you believe it.

- Do you keep reminding yourself of it?
- Do you pick away at it like a scab?
- Do you keep repeating these names to yourself over and over again so you end up believing they are true?

Jesus wants you to leave this lie behind. You don't want to take it with you where you are going in life.

But if you choose to keep believing it, you won't be free to live in the confidence of being God's daughter.

Once you have written it down, stick it to the bottom of your shoe and walk it off or bury it in the garden! Crush that name under your feet and, as you do so, remember that those lies don't need to stick to you.

You are free.

> *If God's son sets you free, you are free indeed!*   (John 8:36)

Chapter Three
Uggs in the Rain

What do you do when it suddenly starts to rain?

Some people put their hoods up or grab a brolly. Others dart into a shop or bus shelter. People in a rush might hold a bag or book above their head. The brave ones carry on regardless. In the end everyone gets wet – just to a different degree.

Why are most people so desperate to avoid getting wet? Well, it can make your hair frizz, and if you're wearing Ugg boots (or imitation boots like mine) they stink when they are wet! But, beyond that, what is the big deal? It's just a bit of water.

Have you ever not cared how wet you got? Your friends were shouting at you to come inside but you weren't listening. You were enjoying the amazing feeling of getting soaked and not caring what anyone thought!

When was the last time you dared to live differently?

Girl Power

Friends.

What would your life be like without good friends?

Recently I spent an afternoon with two girls who had been best friends for years, but their friendship was in trouble. The week before, they had both gone to a party, where one of them had lost her virginity. The girl who had had sex was scared she might be pregnant, so I took them both down to the Family Planning Clinic for an STI and pregnancy test. While we were waiting for the nurse, we got chatting. I was concerned that they were both too young to be going all the way with boys, so I said, 'Girls, I just want to make sure that you weren't pressured into having sex when you didn't want it.' The girl who was waiting to have the tests replied, 'He didn't make me do it, or anything. I just wanted to lose my virginity and get it out of the way. My friend [and she pointed to her best friend sitting next to her] said she lost her virginity last year and that I was the only girl in Year 10 not to have done it yet. So I did, and at least now I can say that I am not a virgin any more.'

All the time she was speaking I noticed that her friend was looking more and more uncomfortable.

'Are you OK?' I asked the friend. 'You look a bit awkward.'

After a while she spoke and said something that pretty much ended the friendship.

She turned to her friend who was waiting for a pregnancy and STI test and said, 'I'm really sorry, but I lied to you. I haven't had sex yet. I'm still a virgin. I didn't know you would go ahead and sleep with that guy.'

Can you imagine what the atmosphere was like in that waiting room?

Sometimes the biggest pressures on us don't come from our worst enemies but from our best friends. Maybe you don't feel pressure like this from your friends, but you sometimes find yourself behaving in different ways depending on which group of friends you are with.

Double Trouble

Chloë lived a bit of a double life.

To her church friends, she was a great Christian girl: really caring, a good listener and a great singer in the youth worship band. To her schoolmates she was a wild child: up for anything, popular with all the lads and a great laugh when she was drunk. For a while, Chloë managed to be brilliant at both lives. She felt guilty about it, but she also loved how younger girls at church looked up to her and how friends at school wanted to be her.

But then it all began to unravel.

Months of trying to please everyone and not get caught out took its toll. Things began to go wrong and she didn't know who she could open up to about it. She ended up exhausted, disillusioned and lonely. Worst of all, she didn't really know who the real 'Chloë' was. She had a couple of weeks of doing nothing and just stayed in bed. She thought she had lost herself, her friends and, worst of all, God.

It took a while for Chloë to realize that the only way she could be free to be herself was to stop living a double life. No-one could do this for her: she had to make some choices and be real with people about what was going on.

She lost some friends when she decided to stop going along with the crowd.

She lost some people's trust when she confessed what had been happening.

But it wasn't the end of the world.

And after a while she began to realize not only who the real Chloë was but also who her real friends were. In choosing to listen to what God said about her identity, she had to make some sacrifices. Even though it was hard to do, Chloë made the right choice.

How Smelly Are You?

After a while you become a bit like the people you spend the most time with. You pick up some of their attitudes and ideas without always realizing it. Have you ever been in a room with people who are smoking, or been in a kitchen where something spicy is cooking? When you leave and meet other people, what can they smell on you? Your clothes soak up the smells of cigarettes or food. You might not want the smell to stick to you, but it does.

There are people who will rub off on you in good and bad ways. Parents or friends who know you really well might even be able to tell who you have been with because of how you are behaving. I had a friend who made me feel inferior to him. Whenever I was around him he found ways of pointing out my mistakes. I ended up having to toughen myself up so that I didn't get hurt. Have a think for a moment: what kind of attitude do you pick up from the people you spend time with?

What are the things they are picking up from you?

Whose attitude would you like to be picking up?

Life to the Max

The disciples spent three solid years picking up a whole new way of living from Jesus. They saw him perform miracles, cast out demons, raise the dead, rescue a boring wedding reception, feed thousands of hungry people and, on top of all this, Jesus showed them what it really meant to be everything that God had made them to be. He told them that he wanted to help them live life to the full.

He still wants to do that for you.

He was once asked by a very clever bloke what he thought was the best way to live life. Jesus answered by asking him what God's law said about it.

> The man answered Jesus, 'Love the Lord your God with all your heart, all your soul, all your strength and all your mind.' And, 'Love your neighbour as yourself.'
> 'Right!' Jesus told him. 'Do this and you will live.'

(Luke 10:27–28)

Imagine if the goal of your life was to live like that!

God asks you, as his daughter, not only to receive his love for yourself, but to pass it on to others. We use the word 'love' to cover a variety of feelings we have for a variety of people and things. The New Testament uses different

Greek words to talk about different types of love. 'Eros' is the sexual love we have for a husband or wife. 'Philia' is the brotherly or sisterly love we feel for family or close friends, hence our word 'filial'. But the word used to describe the love God shows us is 'agape'. Here is a description of this kind of love:

> *Love is patient and kind. Love is not jealous or boastful or proud or rude. Love does not demand its own way. Love is not irritable, and it keeps no record of when it has been wronged . . . love never gives up, never loses faith, is always hopeful, and endures through every circumstance.*
>
> (1 Corinthians 13:4–7)

This love is the never-ending, unconditional, self-sacrificing love that God has for everyone he has made – and he wants us to love like that too!

How does that make you feel?

Could you love your friends, family, even strangers, with this kind of love?

Imagine what might happen if you did.

Imagine if you cared more about people experiencing God's love through you than you did about what people thought about you.

Mother Teresa was an incredible woman who spent her whole life caring for very poor and sick people in Calcutta, India. She would wash stinking bodies, cuddle children who were dying of AIDS and show unending love and respect to people who had lost everything. Many celebrities rush in and out of these places and show 'love' in small and glamorous bursts. But Mother Teresa chose to love like this day in and day out. It must have been incredibly costly to live this way. She said the following about why she chose to love people even when it was hard:

> *The success of love is in the loving – it is not in the result of loving. Of course it is natural in love to want the best for the other person, but whether it turns out that way or not does not determine the value of what we have done . . . We think sometimes that poverty is only being hungry, naked and homeless. The poverty of being unwanted, unloved and uncared for is the greatest poverty. We must start in our own homes to remedy this kind of poverty.*
>
> (Mother Teresa)

Whole families and communities can be changed by the loving actions of ordinary people like you and me. Do you want to be part of changing this world? Then the answer is simply this: love your friends, love your family and love your neighbours.

Are you prepared to live and love like this?

Even if people think you are being a bit odd or they misunderstand your motives, could you still show love?

Could this be the big thing that God wants for your life?

> *I have always wanted my life to count for something – for God. It didn't have to be a 'big' thing – just something. I wanted to do something for Him that no one else on earth would do.*
>
> *From deep inside me I wanted to please God and not let Him down. That was even more important than trying to fit in with my friends.*

I really struggled, aged thirteen, in my first year at secondary school. I was terrified of getting things wrong. I felt I had no friends, and wasn't ever going to fit in. My daughter finds that hard to believe, as now (aged thirty-eight) I have a fantastic group of amazing friends! But at secondary school, because I felt lonely and afraid, I really took hold of my faith for myself – instead of just going along with it because of my parents.

I really started to pray – very simple chats with God – and as a result learned to feel and know that God is with me in every situation. That helped me loads and from that time I have known that I am never, ever alone. It's never just me trying to get through this life, but it's always me and God. So cling on to Him.

Although it was a very difficult time, I can see that the experience then still helps me now. I am aware of people around who perhaps feel that they don't 'fit in', or feel lonely, and try to help. I do believe that many of the hard times God helps us through – at some point we will then meet others who need help too.

(Julie Wilkins, mum of a teenage girl)

I pray that there will be many godly girls around the world who get their boots on (Uggs or otherwise), get out there and dare to live differently!

Wonder_land

- Have you ever put up with an unhappy friendship because you didn't want to be alone or left out?
- 'As a teenager I was so caught up with me and my world! I was concerned about being overlooked and not appreciated for who I was as a person among friends and boys. I did get over-occupied

with comparing myself to other people. I would use my female peers who appeared clever, or attractive or outgoing and popular as my measuring stick for success. How I was matching up to them could often determine how I felt about myself on any given day' (Emily, youth worker and mum).

- Who do you compare yourself with? There is a difference between comparing yourself with someone and admiring them. Who do you admire and look up to?
- What kind of attitudes do you pick up from the people you spend most of your time with? Whose attitude would you like to be picking up?
- Are there people you need to show love to in practical ways (such as doing the washing up, taking out the rubbish, being a listening ear)?
- What might happen if you and your friends made a habit of noticing the people whom everyone else ignores? Don't think that you need to go to a different country before you can begin to make a difference. Who are the people in your school or street who need to know that God loves them through the actions of people like you?
- Thousands of years ago the Israelites were told to remind themselves every day about the way God wanted them to live. If you are choosing to live for God and express his love even in difficult situations, what could you do to keep reminding yourself that you belong to him and want to live his way?

You shall love the Lord your God with all your heart, with all your soul, and with all your strength. Keep these words that I am commanding you today in your heart. Recite them to your children and talk about them when you are away, when you lie down and when you rise. Bind them as a sign on your hand, fix them as an emblem on your forehead, and write them on the doorposts of your house and on your gates.

(Deuteronomy 6:4–9)

My Sanctuary

Do you know who is playing an influential role in your life? Now is your chance to take a few moments to reflect on who you are trying to be like. We all have people we look up to and on the whole this can be a really good thing, but we often don't realize that we can decide how much influence they have on us. You may need to chat through what you discover with someone, especially if you feel the need to change how much time you spend with people.

Write your name in the bubble on the next page. At the end of each line, write the name of someone in your life. It could be a friend, a parent, a member of your wider family, a teacher, a neighbour, etc. Write a name rather than 'family' or 'friends' at the end of each line.

Once you have done this, draw a box around the name of anyone who you would go to for good advice.

Draw a circle around the name of anyone who makes you feel inadequate/ who you compare yourself with.

Draw a triangle around the name of anyone you admire or feel supported by.

Your name

Take a look at your piece of paper. Is there anything you need to do as a result of this activity? If you feel there is someone in your life who has too much of a negative influence on you, what can you do about it? The best place to start is to ask God to give you strength and find an adult who will help you.

I started the chapter asking you what you do when it rains. Well, next time it rains, run out into it, put your head back and enjoy the feeling of rain falling all over your hair and face!

Chapter Four
First-time Club

I had fancied him all week and he had checked me out once.

Once!

We were at a youth camp, and on the very first day I had spotted this gorgeous boy. He was sporty, popular and totally unaware of me. I tried all the standard girly things I had at my disposal to get his attention: I ignored him, chatted up his mates, and sulked. After the fifth day of trying unsuccessfully to get his attention I was ready to give up, but I had reckoned without the final night's party.

Every event has one: that brilliant moment when it is dark, you are all overly emotional and you realize you aren't going to see each other again. We were planning a midnight walk and bonfire, and I couldn't wait!

That night was really cold, so I wrapped up in layers of warm clothing. My friends had deserted me because I was lovesick and moping. As I sat, alone, gazing into the dying embers of the fire, I felt someone touch my back. I sat really still, not wanting to stop what was happening because it felt strange but nice at the same time. Whoever it was began to move their hand up and down my back (on top of all the layers of jumpers!). Eventually I turned to see who it was, and it was him!

I still remember how I felt.

One thing led to another and in the shadows by the fire I had my first kiss.

Wow.

When we got back to the tents I thought that everyone would be able to tell what had just happened. I felt so different and grown-up!

I wonder how many 'first times' you have had recently?

It could be your first taste of some outrageous food such as snails, or your first time going on holiday with friends. Some 'first times' can make you feel really proud and you want to tell everyone: 'I passed my driving test!' 'I got an A in French!' 'I stood up for myself for the first time!' 'Last night I became a sister!'

Other 'first times' we try to keep from people, especially our parents: 'I got my first piercing somewhere other than my ears!' 'I tried my first cigarette.' 'I told my mum I was revising with friends when in fact we were in town – it's the first time I've lied to her like that.'

I remember the first time I chose to talk to my friends rather than my mum about what was going on in my life. I began to keep secrets from her and not find it so easy to open up.

That was a big first for my mum too.

When I was little I told her everything, and when I started being secretive about my thoughts she felt that I didn't need her in my life. She hadn't done anything to make me not trust her; it was just that at the time it felt more important to talk to my girlfriends about things.

One of the best things you can do is realize that you don't need to choose between your friends and your mum or another adult you love and trust. Things change in your life and you experience new situations and feelings, so you need your mum and older women around you. Friends can be great at listening and caring, but older women are often better at giving good (if at times difficult) advice. As hard as it is to believe, your mum or carer has probably been through some of the things you are facing. If you really can't talk to her, then go and find an older woman who can be a bit like a mum to you. There are loads of women out there at your school or church who will be great at supporting you. It will make them feel special that you want to confide in them.

Girl Talk

All our 'first times' remind us that we are growing up and changing. It is an exciting and confusing process that all of us go through.

Have you noticed yourself being a nightmare daughter and an amazing friend at the same time?

Have you noticed yourself falling in love with a boy and falling out with a mate before the end of the first lesson?

What's going on? In a word, you are going through puberty, which means you are on the road to becoming an adult. This isn't an excuse for being a nightmare to your family, but it does explain why you feel as if you are on an emotional roller coaster!

Some of the changes that happen during puberty are obvious:

- Your sweat glands start working and producing body odour (that smell we all get embarrassed by!).
- You get hair around your vagina and under your arms and thicker hair on your legs.
- You put on a bit of weight, especially around your tummy and hips (this happens to every girl, so don't go on a diet).
- Your breasts begin to develop (when this happens, you need to get a bra).
- Your sex organs start to grow (vagina, cervix, womb, fallopian tubes).
- Your ovaries start releasing an egg each month (this means that if you had sex you could get pregnant).
- Your period starts (to begin with, it lasts a few days and is a dark brown colour).
- Your body shape changes and you get taller.

Our bodies are complicated. Some of these physical changes can feel pretty exciting, while others can take us by surprise!

Too often, we forget how incredible and fragile our bodies actually are. The mere fact that you are alive, right now, with all your vital organs working, is a miracle. At the point of your conception, there were millions of sperms making their way towards an egg to fertilize it. Any of those sperms could have got there first, but didn't. One sperm fertilized one egg at the right time to make you.

You are quite literally one in a million.

Getting to know how your body works can let you in on a few secrets of how you are doing. For example, a headache might tell you that you need to drink more water or go to bed earlier. A stomach ache might tell you that you are feeling a bit nervous about something.

But growing up isn't just about what happens to your body. You also find yourself dealing with new emotions, different situations and the challenges of maturing into a young woman.

When I reached puberty and started my periods I felt a bit overwhelmed with loads of emotions I hadn't really felt before. I got embarrassed or offended by the smallest things and sometimes I would fly off the handle at my family for no reason. I wanted people to notice me and think I was pretty, but I didn't like people staring at me. Do you know what I am talking about?

Puberty affects everyone in different ways. I started my periods later than lots of my friends. I also didn't grow very big breasts, and have to confess that there were times when I stuffed loo roll down my bra to boost my confidence! I don't advise it, though. Just imagine what would happen if it rained.

In her diary, written during the Second World War, Anne Frank described her period as a 'sweet secret'.[1] Even though it was uncomfortable, even painful at times, she was glad that she had it because it showed she wasn't a little girl any more.

What a beautiful thing to say about growing into a young woman. It's not the kind of thing you normally hear girls say. But it's true. The journey that you are on through puberty is really precious, and it matters to God.

Sweet Secret

In some ancient cultures, when women had their monthly period (at the same time as each other because they lived in close community) they had a few girly days without the guys around, just enjoying the fact that they were different from men and sharing being women together. They would massage each other's feet and backs and chat about love. Young women who started their periods would be welcomed into the 'womanhood' or the 'Red Tent' with songs and lots of pampering. Women don't do this today, but I thought that I would ask some of my girl mates (of all ages) to share their advice not only about how to survive having periods each month, but also how to thrive as a woman!

'Even though you won't feel like it, do some exercise. Even just stretching your legs will lessen the cramps you get' – Sally

'You are going to have your period for the next thirty years (on and off), so keep a healthy perspective and find your own ways of dealing with it. It doesn't need to take over your life. When my period starts each month I try and welcome it, as it reminds me that my body is able to create new life' – Jenny

'Accidents do happen, and sometimes periods arrive unexpectedly. Don't panic, though, because no-one will notice. I am a high-school teacher and girls are always coming to me and saying that they have leaked and all the boys will notice. The fact is that boys aren't tuned in to this stuff and they don't notice – most of them don't really know what a period is! If you can, keep an emergency kit (like a pencil-case-sized bag) in your school bag with clean knickers and sanitary towels. Periods are an excuse for support from female teachers – but use this excuse wisely!' – Katy

'Whenever I get my period I fill up my hot-water bottle and snuggle on the couch with a bit of chocolate. I feel better in no time!' – Gabriella

'Even if your period hurts a bit, remember that periods are part of becoming a woman and maybe one day becoming a mum. That's a miracle!' – Jo

'Buy a calendar or diary and make a note each month when you have your period. This will help you realize why you are feeling a bit under the weather' – Lizzie

'Each month when you have your period you will think that people will be able to notice or that you will be more smelly than usual. Just wash each day as normal and try not to go overboard on body spray. Some girls get told that periods are dirty things or that it is bad blood. This isn't true at all. Having a period is a precious part of being a woman. It is private but it is also special. Don't hate it and don't hate your body as you grow up. You are beautiful!' – Kellie

Growing Up Is About . . .

At the same time as experiencing some of the awkward things about growing up, you have probably noticed that you feel more passionately about issues you come across. You might get moved to tears watching the news or you might want to campaign about child poverty, animal welfare, environmental issues or some injustice that has really got you fuming.

These new feelings and responses are just as important as everything that happens to your body physically. Building a strong character and growing in compassion for the world you see around you is a crucial part of being God's daughter. The older you get, the more you realize that life isn't perfect and that you have a part to play in bringing God's love and hope to the world.

So how would you sum up your own 'growing-up' experience?

If you wrote a list of things that explained what growing up is all about for you, what would you include?

Here are some of my ideas of what growing up is all about:

- Getting better at thinking twice before doing something you might later regret.
- Not feeling so self-conscious about how you look.
- Knowing what you are into and passionate about.
- Being more private about your stuff and some of your thoughts.
- Learning how to negotiate with your parents about things like bedtime, pocket money, staying out . . . and not always getting it right!
- Getting more and more eager to live like Jesus.
- Taking responsibility for yourself and the things you do.
- Still needing your parents or carers but in different ways (you don't need them to do everything for you but you still need to have

  people you trust who can help you make wise choices about who
  you hang out with, what courses you take or what job you go for).
- Recognizing your emotions and not letting them control you.
- Knowing that if you break up with friends in the heat of the
  moment, you can make up with them when you have cooled down.
- Thinking for yourself, even if your opinion is different from other
  people's.
- Working at relationships with your family and friends and not just
  giving up on people when the going gets tough.
- Listening to God for yourself and asking him to speak to you.
- Making mistakes and then realizing that it isn't the end of the world
  and you can pick yourself up and start again.
- Growing bolder and more confident in who you are and what you
  believe in.
- Involving God in your friendships and relationships.

One of the marks of growing up is that people expect more from you. Have you noticed that? Parents rightly expect you to do more around the house and take responsibility for your stuff as well as your actions. Teachers at school expect you to take responsibility for your own learning and don't regularly check that you are OK as they did when you were younger. You have more freedom to choose what to wear, who to hang out with, what to believe, etc. But simply getting older doesn't automatically mean that people make good choices – that requires maturity and wisdom.

Immaturity means caring only about yourself and how *you* feel. When we live only for ourselves, our actions and choices eventually let us down. Instead of making our lives better and deeper, we end up being controlled by our jealousy, envy, greed, bitterness and selfishness. In the end we need rules in our homes, schools and societies to stop us all from hurting each other through our selfish choices and actions.

Because God made us he knows that, left to our own devices, we tend to mess things up. That's why God gives us the beautiful gift of his Holy Spirit. When we have God's Spirit in us, we begin to think and live differently.

The Holy Spirit isn't a magic formula that means we can do and think only nice things! Instead, God's Spirit helps us to grow to be more compassionate, trusting, patient, loving and passionate for God, like Jesus. These are God-like qualities that we show when we choose to live for Jesus, and the Bible calls them the 'fruits of the Spirit'. They are things such as 'love, joy, peace, patience, kindness, generosity faithfulness, gentleness and self-control' (Galatians 5:22–23). When people's choices are controlled by these things, we don't need rules to stop us from hurting each other.

There is so much about growing up that can feel totally out of our control (getting taller, having spots, feeling self-conscious). We need to remember that the goal of growing up isn't simply to be older and taller. Our aim is to become more and more like Jesus every day. This is what growing up well means.

> *We can rejoice too, when we run into problems and trials, for we know that they are good for us – they help us learn to endure. And endurance develops strength of character in us, and character strengthens our confident expectation of salvation. And this expectation will not disappoint us. For we know how dearly God loves us, because he has given us the Holy Spirit to fill our hearts with his love.*

(Romans 5:3–5)

So as your limbs lengthen,
as your hair grows longer and your body changes shape,
as hormones race through your body waking you up to womanhood,
may you know that Jesus is working in you his great and perfect plan.
May you begin to look more and more like him so that your life brings
hope and blessing to the world.

Wonder_land

- What first times have you had recently? How did you feel about them? Is there anyone you would like to talk to about them?
- What are you enjoying about growing up?
- What are you *not* enjoying so much about growing up?
- How is your character changing and developing as you grow older? If you can't answer this, then ask someone who has known you for a while.
- If you wrote your own list about what growing up is all about for you, what would it include? Why not write down some of your ideas?
- If you have already started your periods and you are able to, get hold of a diary or a calendar. Make a mark on the days when you are having your period. Put a 'P' in a circle on the days you are on. This will help you begin to predict when your next period is due to start. Pharmacists and doctors can help if your period pains are very painful or mood swings are very strong. If you haven't started your periods yet, don't worry! Everyone is different. Think about what you feel about periods. Tell the doctor or pharmacist about your concerns, and ask them questions. This will help you face starting your periods with a more confident attitude.

How well are you growing up?

How mature and wise are you?

The activity below is intended to help you reflect on how you see your life choices and responsibilities. Look at the dartboard design on the next page. In the outer ring, write down choices or issues that you feel you have no control over (e.g. pollution/being a girl, etc.). In the second circle, write down the choices you have limited control over (e.g. going to school/ who you hang out with/what you eat), and in the middle circle, write down choices you have complete control over (e.g. what to say/taking drugs, etc.).

Look over what you have written and ask yourself these questions:

- What choices have I made today?
- What is the difference between a good choice and a bad choice?
- Do my choices end up hurting me and other people?

There are so many pressures and changes for you to cope with as you grow into adulthood. If you really want to grow up well then you need God's help. The wonderful truth is that, because he made and loves you, he is the best person to help you grow into the woman he wants you to be.

When the Holy Spirit controls our lives, he will produce this kind of fruit in us: love, joy, peace, patience, kindness, goodness, faithfulness, gentleness, and self-control.

(Galatians 5:22–23)

In this still and safe place, speak to God. It is possible to change how you act and behave. It comes from a heart full of the love of God and a life full of the Spirit of God. Why not invite God to fill you with his Spirit?

Chapter Five
Holy Body

Lycra-wonder!

When I was fifteen I had a very significant run-in with my dad. I remember the night quite vividly.

I had got into the habit of leaving my parents' house to go out with friends wearing one outfit, and then changing into something I thought was way 'more sexy' when I got to their house. The more I did this, the more risks I took, and one evening I thought, 'What the heck, I can slip on my tight lime-green Lycra® trousers and boob tube and sneak out of the front door without being caught!'

All was going well until the unexpected happened. I had my hand on the front door latch when all of a sudden my dad (who must have been listening out for me) threw open the lounge door and caught me sneaking out of the house in full Lycra® splendour! I shut my eyes and waited for my dad to lay into me and pronounce that from henceforth I would be grounded for life.

But he surprised me.

He just looked at me and said, 'Rachel, you're my best and only daughter. I'm really proud of you and hope you have a great night.'

That was it!

I was stunned.

No shouting, no lecture, no grounding. I was free to go!

As I walked out of the house, something inside me clicked. I looked at what I was wearing and felt as cheap as the fabric it was made of. I turned round, went back to my room and changed into something else.

My dad had reminded me that I was precious to him. That he loved and cherished me. It made me feel so warm and special and it changed that night for me.

I still had times when I wore really revealing clothes. I still wanted the boys to look at me. But from that moment on I knew for sure that my dad thought I was beautiful and I didn't need to prove myself to anyone else.

God your Father created you to be beautiful – and that's what you are! He made your heart, mind and soul – and he also created your body. You don't need to keep it hidden away under layers of cardigans or tracksuits. You also don't need to put it on display to try to entice boys to take a second look at you. Instead, God wants you to accept, appreciate and value your body.

Classy Cars

Have you ever seen an advert on TV for a Porsche or a Mercedes Benz?

No?

Why is that?

It's probably because that kind of top quality doesn't need to advertise itself. The car's value speaks for itself and only people who have a lot of cash can buy it.

The kind of cars you do see advertised on TV are cars that are a bit like all the others. There is nothing extra special or flash about them. If they want to sell them, their makers have to do all they can to get the customers' attention and persuade them that this is a car worth owning.

Open any magazine and you will see photos of and articles on women who are convinced that they need to prove that they are worth something by making themselves look sexy and available. Their clothing is tight, their skin is flawless, their boobs are on display and their facial expressions say, 'Come and use me; I'm all yours.'

Is this what it means to accept and appreciate your body?

Does loving your body mean getting everyone else to love your body too?

Do you have value as a human being only if someone thinks you look sexy?

No!

But, sadly, being sexy seems to be the goal of many girls' lives. They want every boy to fancy them and every girl to envy them. Only this way do they feel that they are worth having, and unfortunately they often end up giving themselves to any guy who wants them. Rather than making them feel more valuable, this kind of behaviour actually ends up leaving them feeling used up and worthless.

If we treat ourselves as sex objects, it's hardly surprising if guys do too.

Opposites Attract

But the alternative to being a sex object is not to dress in bin liners from head to foot!

You don't need to be afraid of the fact that boys like girls' bodies. You just need to make sure that the clothes you wear and the way you wear them help boys see that there is more to you than meets the eye.

Our bodies play a powerful role in attraction and intimacy. Often the first thing you notice about a boy is how he looks, but it's more than just whether he is 'hot' or not. Have you noticed how your friends might be attracted to different-looking lads from you? This is because someone's looks are more than what their face or hair is like. What you are attracted to is the combination of their personality, their facial expression and the way they talk, walk, smile or treat people.

Being attracted to the opposite sex is a good thing. Our world depends on men and women falling in love, committing themselves to each other, having sex and raising families that ensure the human race doesn't die out.

As we get older, the way we are attracted to people begins to change. As our bodies grow we begin to notice each other in more sexual ways. We notice a good-looking girl who walks by and compare ourselves with her.

We notice a good-looking guy and wonder if he has noticed us. We quickly learn that there are some things we can do to make a guy take a second look!

What's on the Menu?

I remember leaving home to go to university when I was nineteen and being terrified. I was pretty convinced that no-one would like me and I don't think I had ever cooked myself a proper meal in my life (I have an awesome mum!), so I was dreading the prospect of having to look after myself. But, within days, I soon discovered that I wasn't the only person with food on their mind.

One morning, as my friend and I were packing our bags to leave the class, an older guy from our course leant over, looked us up and down and said, 'Girls, men might be on a diet, but they still check out the menu.' What was that all about? And what a creep! We couldn't quite believe what we had heard.

Was it a cheap chat-up line or an insult?

What did it mean that men 'still checked out the menu'? *What* menu?

We talked about it for days.

Let's Hear It from the Boys

It isn't OK for guys (of any age) to check out girls in a rude way and make suggestive comments about what they look like, but I suppose this is where we girls have to face a bit of a reality check. Even though we aren't always aware of it, the way that we dress does send out signals to men. They are curious about girl's bodies, so when more flesh is on display (low-cut tops, short shorts, tight clothes, etc.) they are immediately drawn to take a look.

I thought I would do a bit of research, so I asked a few of my male friends if they could throw a bit of light on the subject. I asked them this question: 'Does a girl's choice of clothing affect a boy's attitude towards her?' Here are some of their answers:

SAM:
'Boys view looking at girls as a bit of a game. If you see a girl that's dressed up in a sexy way (tight clothes, low-cut top), then it's an encouragement to go and chat her up. She might as well have a sign over her head saying, "Come over here, boys, I'm easy!" It's like it's a green light. Whatever a girl chooses to wear will affect how a boy chats to her.'

MAURO:
'I would be lying if I said that I didn't like looking at girls, but, please, sometimes you make it really hard for a guy to get to know you when things are hanging out! Most guys see girls as either girlfriend material or just a bit of easy fun. I know girls don't like that, but it's true. Girls who dress in a really easy way aren't girlfriend material in most guys' eyes.'

JASON:
'As baby boys, lads spend the first few months of our life dependent on breasts, so that's why there is a strong hangover attraction for blokes to women's breasts. A man might be drawn to a woman because of her breasts, but he won't stay with her because of them!'

So what do we girls think about this? Is it our fault that boys get so quickly turned on by what they see? That's their responsibility, isn't it?

I asked a few of my girlfriends for their response.

KATY:
'I always knew that guys LOVE women's bodies and find prettty much anything a turn-on. I think that it is both of our responsibilities to make sure that we don't get driven by our urges and end up regretting things. I know that I get more attention from guys at parties if I wear tight clothes, but I don't really want that kind of attention. I am not exactly going to be sending out the message that I could be a great girlfriend if everything about how I look screams, "I am anyone's"!'

NICKY:
'Some girls wear their clothes in a really sexy way and then wonder why they are getting a lot of attention from guys. They also find that sometimes the guys who give them attention are not always the guys they want to attract. They might find a guy who will be interested in them for the night, but the next day he is off looking for someone else. The easier you make it for him to get what he wants, the less effort he has to make to be with you. In the end this means that it is easier for him to move on and get together with someone else.'

So how aware are you of how your clothes and the way you wear them affect guys? Have you been a bit naive about things and not taken responsibility for how you look?

In 'God Part 2' by U2, from the album *Rattle and Hum*, Bono sings about how, despite not believing in forced entry or rape, when a boy sees a girl the temptations can be very powerful. Bono's lyrics are quite shocking.

He warns us that we mustn't underestimate just how much of a turn-on a bit of cleavage or bare skin can be for a boy, even one who is a really good mate. This doesn't mean that you should dress in a duvet cover from the neck down, to stop boys getting turned on by you. But you need to realize that if you want lads to think of you as more than a sex object, then you need to dress in a way that sends out that signal. In reality, girls who dress in a way that shows they respect themselves and their bodies tend to be more attractive and appealing to a guy in the long run because there is an air of mystery about them. They aren't easy, they don't go with just anyone – and that can be fascinating for the lads.

Before we go any further, it is really important that we understand that it is OK to like how people look and to enjoy getting a bit of attention.

It's OK to like looking at boys.

It's OK to like boys looking at you.

What you need to do is ask yourself whether you put too much emphasis on lads looking at you.

Some girls like attention from boys but know that in the end it can be a bit like sunbathing. It's OK to begin with, but if you do it for too long you will end up getting burnt!

Other girls need boys to be looking at them before they can feel pretty or special. That's a problem because it shows that they don't really know who they are and what makes them special. Loving someone and fancying them are two very different things. Sometimes girls end up having sex with a guy who fancies them because they mistake this for love. They often feel even more unloved as a result.

No amount of hot guys looking at you will make you feel loved and special. The author Nigel Pollock says, 'The value we try and earn is always a lot less than the value we already have.'[1] This means that the way people see us or treat us doesn't make us more or less special. It can change how we feel about ourselves, but it can't change the facts about us: our value comes from God, who loves us and never changes his mind about us.

The Body Beautiful

In the Bible, Paul describes our bodies as 'temples'. A temple is a sacred and holy place where God lives. Another translation for the word 'temple' is 'sanctuary'.

> *Do you not know that your body is a temple of the Holy Spirit within you, which you have from God, and that you are not your own? For you were bought with a price; therefore glorify God with your body.*
> (1 Corinthians 6:19–20)

The greatest price has been paid for us, body and soul. Jesus came to earth as a human being, lived among a group of people in Israel and gave up his life for everyone so that we can be free from everything that separates us from God.

When Paul was writing to the Christians in Corinth, people believed that the way to be happy and free was to do whatever you wanted with your body: binge-drink, eat to excess, have sex with anyone – even in the temple! Corinth was full of temples to Greek gods and goddesses that encouraged people to do all this as a way of getting closer to 'God'. But, instead of freedom, Paul saw that these people were slaves to their desires: they were ruled by what their body craved.

Paul wrote to the Christians to tell them that they didn't have to do any of these things to get closer to God. God's Spirit was already inside them, making their bodies temples – houses for God! Not only is having sex with anyone outside marriage a big 'no', but having the attitude that 'I can do whatever I want with my body' is also out of the question.

Your body belongs to God, and he wants you to live for him body and soul, free from the obsessions and concerns that preoccupy people who don't know God. You also belong to the body of Christ – men and women all round the world who follow Jesus. Together, we show the world what Jesus is all about – we are his body on earth. So we can't do what we want with our body; it belongs to God, and how we treat it shows people how we feel about him.

This doesn't mean that if you are a Christian God is angry if you go on a diet or get a piercing! But it does mean that everything you feel about your body and do with it matters to God.

Attitude Analysis

What is your attitude to your body? Here are some *unhealthy* attitudes:

> 'If I could change anything about my body, it would be . . . everything!'
> 'All I am is something for guys to look at.'
> 'I look rough unless I put loads of slap on.'
> 'If I lost weight, people would like me more.'
> 'I can't deal with how I am feeling but I feel better about myself when I don't eat anything.'
> 'People can do what they like to me – it's only my body, it isn't the real me.'
> 'When I cut myself I feel so much more in control of my life'.

If you are experiencing any of these things then you need to find someone you trust to share them with. They won't be shocked or angry at what you are doing. They will help you find the right kind of help for you so you can begin to deal with your concerns. There are also some great websites for young people that look at some of these issues, including www.thesite.org; www.firstsigns.org.uk and www.selfharm.co.uk.

Here are some *healthy* attitudes to your body:

> 'I might be shorter than other girls my age but I am really fast – perfect for playing football.'
> 'When I buy clothes I try and find something that suits my body shape rather than try to get what everyone else is wearing. When I feel more comfortable in my clothes, I am more confident.'

'I have a shower regularly and use deodorant spray under my arms. It's good to keep clean and healthy, but not to get obsessed about it.'

'The other day my stomach rumbled in class. I was a bit embarrassed at first but I laughed it off with my friends. It happens to everyone at some point – it's no big deal.'

'I get pretty tired during the week so I try to limit how much TV I watch at night. And I definitely set a time limit in how long I spend on Facebook!'

'I love Indian food! It's great to have a meal out with your friends or family.'

Building a healthy body image is all part of being God's daughter. But the really important thing is not to be hard on yourself if you struggle with this. It isn't easy in a body-obsessed society to hold on to God's perspective of your body and how you should treat it. You must never lose sight of the fact that your beauty comes from your inner spirit. No amount of fashionable clothes or looks to die for can replace the inner strength and confidence that come from knowing God's love and acceptance of you. True beauty comes from within; it shines through your words and actions, it stays with people like a beautiful scent.

You *can* be the girl who knows that, whatever shape she is, her beauty and value come from more than simply how she looks.

You *can* be the girl who helps people discover just how lovely her heart is.

You *can* be the girl who knows that the boy who is worthy of her is prepared to take time to get to know her.

Remember how big a price was paid for you. Use your body to glorify God.

Wonder_land

- Dressing sexily sends out signals to boys about what they will get when they get together with you. What signals do your clothes send out to guys?
- Do you think it is OK for guys and girls to do all they can to make themselves attractive to each other? Where do you think people should draw the line?
- When you get dressed in the morning or for a party, how do you go about choosing your outfit? Do you think about what your clothes are telling people about how you want to be treated? Do you have a close friend you trust who could help you answer that question? And once you have all your glad rags on and check yourself in the mirror one last time, do you look more like yourself or more like someone else?
- What kind of image do you think a daughter of God should have?
- How do you look after your body? Does the way you care for yourself show other people that you value yourself, or do people think you don't care what happens to you? You might need to do a bit of a health check on your attitude to your body. Ask yourself these questions:

How am I feeling: tired? hungry? rested? sad? content? Is there anything that I can do about how I am feeling right now (such as go to bed earlier)?

(If you smoke) do I really want to be a smoker?
Am I eating enough healthy food?

Am I cutting myself to let out the pain rather than finding other ways to deal with my hurts?

Do I tend to focus on the bits of my body I don't like rather than learning to love how I am made?

Do I regularly talk to someone I love and trust about what I am thinking and feeling?

Can I cry when I feel sad, or do I bottle up my feelings?

- As your body is a temple for God's Spirit, what habits or actions does that mean that you should avoid? Who can you talk to about this?
- As your body is a temple for God's Spirit, what things should you be doing with your body to glorify him?

My Sanctuary

As girls, it is really important for us to feel loved and affirmed as a woman by the men in our lives. When we are growing up, the most important man in our life might be our dad, brother, carer or granddad.

If you have a loving dad in your life, why not write him a letter about what his love and support means to you? It will be one of the most important and precious letters he will ever receive.

If you know what it is like to miss out on having a supportive and loving dad, talk about it to your mum or an older woman you trust. Ask yourself how not having your dad around has affected how you feel about yourself.

In our youth centre there are a few older lads who act a bit like big brothers to some of the younger girls. They look out for them, respect them and remind them that they are lovely young women who should look after themselves.

This has really helped a fifteen-year-old girl called Nikita. Her dad walked out on her and her mum last year. Nikita was left feeling hurt and angry. She started going out with much older boys because the older man in her life (her dad) wasn't up to the job of loving and supporting her. When she started coming to our centre she was so amazed that there were older guys around who just wanted to look out for her — they weren't trying to get it on with her.

My friend Bri is a dad to a little girl called Mercy. Here is an extract from a letter he wrote to her when she was 3 years old.

To my little girl, Mercy;

I'll never forget when I first held you.

You were so tiny; your fingers, downy hair, gorgeous blue eyes that were like pools. We stared at each other. You were so lovely, from the first moment I saw you.

Sometimes, dads don't always know what to feel, or what to say, or what to think. Sometimes, dads don't always know what to do. Even if they like to look as if they do.

I don't want to ever think that my love for you came cheap, like a plastic toy from a cornflake packet. There are two things I know for sure; one, that my love will always grow with you, and emerge into the daylight of your life. Two, it will never fade or die.

Today, I love you precisely for who you are; not for who I hope you will become. You will be who you will be. And you are already all that I could possibly hope or imagine.

When you are sad, or lonely, or far off; and when you are crying with laughter, or get carried away without a care, I will love you to the moon and back. Whatever happens, no matter how many times I may need to pick you up or dust you off, or wipe dirt from your hands or snot from your nose or blood from your lips or tears from your eyes, I will hold you tight and squeeze you – to tell you that I am here for you, for as long as I draw breath.

I know that one day I will have to be big and brave enough to let you go. But just for now, let me hold your hand and squeeze it tight.

You are so, so lovely.

And I am yours,

Your

Daddy x

Whatever our dads are like, the most wonderful thing, which is true for all of us, is that our heavenly Father is the best dad the world will ever know. He is always aware of where you are and how you are doing. His love for you is not dependent on your feeling 'like a princess' or being good all the time. He can't help but love you because that is who he is, and he has made you to be loved by him. He is the only one whose love can totally fill our hearts to bursting. In the Bible he describes himself as like a mother hen, gathering all her baby chicks under her wings for safety and protection.

Why not tell your heavenly Father what you are longing for or how you are feeling?

He's listening.

Magic Mirror

There was once a girl who was given a magic mirror for her birthday. Whenever she gazed into its depths she could ask for one wish to be granted.

But this mirror was not only magic – it was greedy as well.

In return for granting a wish, the mirror demanded something from the girl that was uniquely hers and no-one else's.

The girl considered this for a while and then agreed. After all, the mirror could give her all she could ever wish for.

So the girl and the magic mirror began their daily exchange. In return for new clothes, DVDs and popularity at school, the mirror demanded a lock of the girl's hair, an ornament she made for her mum when she was six, her first-ever Valentine's card.

The partnership was perfect.

But the girl began to wish for more, and, as her greed increased, so did the mirror's.

The girl demanded more complicated favours: long hair that never frizzed; a boyfriend who would never look at another girl; to be the most famous and wealthy woman in the world.

In return for granting such outrageous requests, the mirror demanded ever-larger pay-offs, but the girl was quickly running out of objects to trade that were uniquely hers. In her greed and desperation she began to offer the mirror her colourful imagination, her crazy sense of humour, her caring personality.

One day, as the girl gazed into the mirror with a wish on her lips, she realized in horror that she had nothing left of herself to give. She begged and pleaded with the mirror to take pity on her and grant her final wish – but the mirror was silent.

Over the years the girl's looks began to wither, her fame began to fade and her friends moved away. In giving away all that was uniquely hers, she was left to fade away like a shadow.

The End.

Chapter Six
The Invisible Girl

Stuff

I hate losing stuff. But unfortunately I have a habit of doing just that. Yesterday I lost my phone and found it in my bed.

The other week I lost my house keys and found them the next day in the bottom of a bag that I was convinced I had checked.

When I lose stuff I drive everyone mad by storming round the house and turning everything upside down until I find what I've lost. But it isn't only things that we can lose. On the whole, they can be replaced. But what happens when you lose something that's harder to get back, such as:

A good feeling
Confidence
A sense of where you are heading in life
Your closest friend
Popularity
The trust of your parents
The love of a boyfriend
Hope
Your own self-respect
Your reputation?

I don't know if you have ever lost anything on this list.

I don't know what regrets you have.

A Million Steps

Nicky knew all about regrets. Standing outside the youth centre in Florida, she looked at me and sighed, 'I wish someone had told me this stuff when I was younger. I'd have done things differently.'

I know how Nicky felt that night. She was fifteen, far from her home in North London, and had just spent a week with a load of other British teenagers listening to 'a bunch of American religious idiots' telling her to hold off from having sex with her boyfriend while they talked about other stuff, like what she wanted to do with her life and whether sleeping with him was the best choice to make. She'd been surprised, annoyed even, at how they'd really got to her and shown her how chasing guys all the time was actually making her hurt like crazy.

The result? She was beginning to think about where her life was heading and she didn't particularly like what she saw. Away from her home and friends it hit her how much she lived her life to fit in with others and how little she was thinking about what she was doing and the lasting impact it was going to have on her life. She could see all the millions of steps she had taken in her life that had led to this moment.

And this moment was full of regrets that left her feeling less like herself and very confused. She was not sure where she was heading, but she was

going there at high speed and was afraid that it was too late to do anything about it; she couldn't change direction or speed.

I meet so many girls who regret choices they have made and wish they could go back and do things differently the second time round.

They have got to the point where they have little or no choice over what they do. And they have no idea how they have got there. They don't see the millions of steps they have taken that have led them to that point.

Do you know what I am talking about?

Is there something you do that you feel you have little or no control over?

It could be a negative thought about yourself that you can't help believing. Or maybe you have started doing something you want to stop, but don't know if you can. Like Nicky, you wish you had done things differently and not been so easily led. Like Nicky, you wish you didn't have so many regrets.

The first step in facing the past is to see the difference between having regrets and feeling guilty. It is really healthy to regret behaviour that has hurt us or other people. In admitting our fault and responsibility in the situation (even if there were other people involved who were at fault too), we can learn from it and choose to act differently next time.

Guilt is different.

It is made up of a mixture of shame ('I can't believe what happened; I can't ever tell anyone') and denial ('I won't do it again, I'm fine, I don't need to talk to anyone'). When we feel guilty about something, we bury our head in the sand and hope that the bad feelings will go. We end up making the same mistakes over and over again and wonder why nothing is changing.

Secret Regrets

Have you ever played the game 'Hotter! Colder!'? You might call it something different. It is when someone hides an object in a room while everyone is waiting outside. When you shout 'Ready!' everyone runs in and tries to find it. To help them along, the person who hid the object shouts, 'Hotter!' or 'Colder!' to let them know how close or far they are to or from finding it.

People who are really good at this game try to throw you off the scent by shouting 'Hotter!' when you are in fact miles away from where the object is hidden!

What are the things that you keep hidden?

Sometimes the need to keep these things hidden can lead to lies. We don't mean to; we just do it because we don't know what might happen if people knew the truth. When people get too close to finding out about our secret, we tell them a lie to send them off in the wrong direction so that we don't get caught out.

But in the end, just as in the game, people will always find it.

The truth will come out.

We keep things hidden for a whole heap of reasons:

- We might feel ashamed of something we have said or done.
- We might feel wrongly ashamed of something that someone has done to us or something about us that is no-one's fault.
- We might be involved in something we know we need to stop but don't feel ready to give up just yet. If we tell someone what's going on they might try to help us to stop, and we don't want them to.
- We might think that it's wrong to have struggles so we don't tell anyone what we are going through because somehow we should be able to cope on our own.
- We don't want to burden other people with our problems: they have got too much to worry about already without us chatting to them about our difficulties.

Keeping something a secret can feel like carrying a very heavy rucksack on our back. Think of any superhero story: the heroes spend all their time hiding their secret identity even from the people they love the most, because they don't know what will happen if people know the truth. Even if they want to be come clean about their real identity, they can't, because they live in a world where people who know the truth about them tend to be killed off!

Do you ever feel like this?

Are there things in your life or heart that are weighing heavily in a 'rucksack' on your back?

Are you afraid of what might happen if people knew about your story?

The Invisible Woman

I heard of a woman who decided to do something about the secret shame she was carrying. For years and years she had been suffering from an illness that made people want to stay well away from her. Friends and family made excuses not to visit and even the religious people in the town wanted nothing to do with her. She felt dirty and worthless.

More recently, she had noticed that, instead of crossing over to the other side of the street when they saw her, people kept on walking, deep in conversation with friends. It was as if they didn't see her at all.

It wasn't such a bad thing not to be noticed. She could sneak around and find out about things. This is how she heard about him, the man who could change everything. She'd heard strange rumours about him: he had made a healing mud that made a blind man see; he'd fed thousands with hardly any food; even the wild weather somehow did what he said. If anyone could help the invisible woman, it was him. If only she could see him, talk to him, touch him.

Later that same day, she got her chance. Turning the corner of the street she found herself in a large crowd of people. Some were crying; others were trying to move people along. Unnoticed, the invisible woman slipped into the middle of the crowd and saw what all the commotion was about. A young man was on his knees, tears streaming down his face, pleading with a dark-skinned stranger to come to his home immediately to heal his dying daughter. In his desperation he was pulling at the stranger's sleeves, begging over and over again, 'Please come, she is dying; only you can help her. Please, *please*!'

The stranger had his back to her, so she couldn't see his face. Was this him? Was this the man who was her last chance to be free from her sickness and shame? It was so hot and the crowd was so loud. The stranger said something to the kneeling man that made him jump up and lead the stranger to his home. The whole crowd surged forward, jostling each other and eager to see what might happen.

'This is it!' thought the invisible woman. 'I have to get to him now before he goes. I might never see him again. If I just touch his coat, maybe that will be enough.'

So she reached out her hand and grabbed Jesus' coat. She managed to hold on to it only for a split second before the crowd behind her pushed her out of the way. Suddenly a loud voice from the middle of the crowd shouted, 'Stop! Who just touched me?'

'What do you mean?' someone asked Jesus. 'Look at this crowd. *Everyone* is touching you!'

'No, someone touched me,' Jesus answered, 'because I felt power leave me. Who was it? I want to see you.'

The woman stood very still, hardly breathing. The crowd looked around, unsure of what was happening. Someone from the dying girl's house arrived to say that she had died; it was too late for Jesus to do anything. People began to cry; others began to get angry about the hold-up. But still Jesus waited.

'Who touched me?' he asked again. 'I want to see who touched me.'

After what felt like an eternity, the invisible woman stepped forward, and Jesus looked at her.

Right there in the middle of the crowded street, in front of people who had forgotten and ignored her, Jesus saw her.

The Bible says that when the woman touched Jesus' coat she was healed from her years of menstrual bleeding. Jesus didn't need to find out who she was. Just touching his cloak healed her suffering. She could have just slipped away from the crowd, still invisible. I wonder if Jesus chose to single her out to let her know that the healing he gave her was not just for her body, but for her whole life. By calling her to step forward into the light, he made sure that she wasn't the invisible woman any more. Not only did he see her for who she was, he made sure that others did too.

If you want to read this story in the Bible for yourself, you will find it in Matthew 9:18–22.

Jesus helps us to see ourselves as we really are. We all need to be forgiven for things we have said and done that have hurt others, us and God. His forgiveness allows us to be set free from our guilt and shame. We have all had different experiences in life. You might be regretting an argument with a friend, or that thing you did that really hurt your mum or carer. Sometimes these things can feel too big to even think about. Jesus can forgive and heal us from all of these.

Virgin Deal

I sometimes chat with girls who have big regrets about sexual experiences. They may have gone too far in a relationship or even had an abortion.

There are some girls who have sexual experiences with older people when they are very young. This is called abuse, and the older person is always in the wrong.

Losing your virginity is when you choose to have an intimately sexual experience with someone. This may be penetrative sex (where the man's penis enters the woman's vagina, often breaking a thin piece of skin at the neck of the womb called the hymen and sometimes causing a little bit of bleeding), or oral sex (where the couple use their mouths on each other's penis or vagina to give them an orgasm). Some people say that losing your virginity isn't just about what you do but about what you are trying to do. So couples who deliberately sexually stimulate each other (touch each other's genitals) are in a bit of a grey area.

Most cultures around the world put a lot more emphasis on the importance of girls being virgins than boys. Girls get gossiped about if they get off with someone or go out with lots of different guys. Boys get congratulated and admired.

There are loads of reasons for this.

Historically, girls from wealthy families were treated a bit like objects that could be traded in marriage to other wealthy or titled families. The promise of their daughter's virginity was evidence of her value and their importance.

It meant that not only had she not had sex, she had also not promised her heart to anyone. She could be bought body, heart and soul. This is not what marriage is about, and it isn't what God's plan of virginity is for.

Some people talk about being a 'technical virgin', which means that they have had a lot of sexual foreplay with someone but stopped short of sexual intercourse. To be honest, I don't think there is such a thing as being a 'technical virgin'. Virginity is a precious gift you have from birth. It's not only your body that is affected by having sex with someone; it is also your heart and spirit. God's plan is that you remain a virgin until you meet the person you will spend the rest of your life getting to know. This is what marriage is and this is why being a virgin before marriage is such a precious gift to save for yourself and your husband. In his first letter to the Christians in Corinth, Paul explains that marriage is the only relationship in which having sex is OK:

> But because there is so much sexual immorality, each man should have his own wife and each woman should have her own husband.
>
> (1 Corinthians 7:2)

And all this talk about virginity is still for you even if you are no longer a virgin.

Some girls think that God loves them less if they have already had sex. It's not true. You will always be precious and lovely in his sight. It is never too late to consider changing your attitudes and future actions. God helps us to make a new start. I don't think that God wants to make you a physical virgin again, but I know that he can heal any guilt you may have in your heart and forgive you for everything you have done. God's love makes you whole and complete. This means you can be confident that you can fall in love and give yourself completely to your future husband without shame.

Some girls find themselves pregnant as a result of having sex. They are faced with a huge decision to make, and many of them can feel very isolated and afraid. Girls who choose to have an abortion can find it very hard to move on and forgive themselves for what has happened. I have seen God heal the broken hearts of girls who have been through this. The Bible tells us that there is nothing we can do that will ever separate us from God and his healing love. Because of what Jesus has done for us, we can know real peace with God and a new beginning in our lives.

> *God showed his great love for us by sending his son to die for us while we were all sinners. And since we have been made right in God's sight by the blood of Christ, he will certainly save us from God's judgement . . . So now we can rejoice in our wonderful new relationship with God – all because of what our Lord Jesus Christ has done for us in making us friends with God.*
>
> (Romans 5:8–11)

You may not have lost your virginity but you might feel that you have got too intimate with someone in a relationship. If you feel guilty about this, then the danger is that you may rush into your next relationship without dealing with what happened in the last one. Take a moment to be honest with yourself about how you acted and how you feel about it. Ask God to forgive you for anything you did that is eating you up. You can't start dating anyone else if you still have unresolved hurts and issues from your last relationship. If you have had any experiences with relationships that you regret, find an adult you trust to talk to about it.

There are some men and women who never marry and never lose their virginity. This can be heartbreaking for those who always wanted to get married. It is so important to remember that no matter how great sex is, it is nothing compared with the love and fulfilment we can find in knowing Jesus and following him.

Jesus said that knowing the truth will set us free from guilt and sin. Jesus called himself 'the way, the truth and the life'. To know him is to know the truth. Knowing him sets us free to live free from dark secrets that make us hide away and wish to be invisible. Even if you feel that other people look at you and fail to see who you really are, you can always be sure that Jesus spots you in the crowd and knows you completely.

Is Jesus asking you to step forward into his light to be set free from past hurts and secrets?

> *Those who look to him are radiant; their faces are never covered with shame.*
>
> (Psalm 34:5, TNIV)

Wonder_land

- What are some of your regrets?
- How do you face your regrets and feeling of guilt?
- Do you sometimes keep things secret that need to come out into the open so that you can face them with support from others?
- Are there times when you feel invisible to people around you? Could it be that you are holding something back from them that they need to be let in on if your relationship with them is going to get any deeper?

- Is Jesus asking you to step forward into his light to be set free from past hurts? If so, find a friend who loves Jesus and step into his light with them. You might want to write these hurts and secrets down and take them outside as a sign that you want to bring them out into the open to let God heal you.

My Sanctuary

If you can, turn the lights low in your room or light some candles. It feels cosy to be in a quiet room with soft lighting and gentle music. This can help you in opening up some of your secret boxes to God. He knows everything about your life, but because he loves you and wants to get a deeper relationship with you, he longs for you to share your fears and dreams with him.

In your head or out loud, invite Jesus to be with you. Listen to what he says to you as you read this poem:

My heart feels like a huge bin stuffed full of memories.
Some are great.
Some are painful.
Whenever I open the lid I have a little rummage
and pick out a few of my favourites;
the teddy bear my first boyfriend gave me,
the last Christmas card from my Granny before she died,
a photo of me and my friends in the summer.
But if I dig too deep I might find memories I don't want to remember;
a broken relationship,
a collection of cruel words my family have said to me,

the way I treated someone I loved.
'Jesus, these are all my memories.
In some way they make me who I am.
When you look through my life, what do you see?
Can you still love me?'
Silence.
A man in the middle of the crowd stops and turns round.
'Who said that?' he asks.
'Who is reaching out for me?
Step forward into the light.'
I take a deep breath,
And I step forward into his light.
He sees me.
I am free.

The Bible is completely hot on the fact that nothing can separate us from God's love. In the book called Romans it says that there is nothing in heaven or on earth that can get in the way of God loving us:

For I am convinced that neither death nor life, neither angels nor demons, neither the present nor the future, nor any powers, neither height nor depth, nor anything else in all creation, will be able to separate us from the love of God that is in Christ Jesus our Lord.

(Romans 8:38–39, TNIV)

Now imagine that God is inviting you to add a few of your own ideas to this passage. What are the things you worry might stop God from loving and cherishing you? Is it the fact that you aren't a virgin? Is it your temper? Your smoking, shopping or gossiping habit? Be brave and write these words in the gaps below. Then read the whole passage out loud and let the truth of God's unconditional love sink in.

> *For I am convinced that nothing can separate me from God's love;*
>
> *neither* _____
>
> *nor* _____ ,
>
> *neither* _____
>
> *nor* _____
>
> *nor anything else in all creation, will be able to separate me from the love of God that is in Christ Jesus our Lord.*
>
> (Romans 8:38–39)

Why not write your own prayer or poem about how you feel about your regrets? You can keep it in a safe place as a reminder that God is with you in the things that others can see and in the deep rooms of your heart that no-one can see.

Chapter Seven
Death to Bad Sex

Sex makes everything complicated. Even when you don't have it, the not having it makes things complicated!

Amanda in *The Holiday*[1]

On a beach there is a ridiculous sign. It reads, 'Do not throw stones at this sign.' That's all it says! It doesn't tell you anything important about the beach; it doesn't give you any information about tide times. It just forbids you to throw stones at a sign that serves no purpose whatsoever except to tell you not to throw stones at it. In fact, it makes you *want* to throw stones at it just because it tells you not to!

Some people think that Christianity is a bit like that sign – all about pointless rules aimed at spoiling their fun. Probably the teaching in the Bible that seems the most strange is that Christians shouldn't have sex before marriage. Some people will even go on to say that the Bible is so strict about sex because it thinks it's dirty or something to be ashamed of.

Nothing could be further from the truth.

The book in the Bible that has the most to say about sex is a book called 'The Song of Solomon' or 'Song of Songs'. Have you ever read it? It's hot stuff! Look at these two sentences:

> *Your two breasts are like twin fawns of a gazelle [a female deer],*
> *feeding among the lilies . . .*
> *You are so beautiful, my beloved, so perfect in every part.*
>
> (Song of Solomon 4:5, 7)

> *My lover tried to unlatch the door, and my heart thrilled within me.*
> *I jumped up to open it. My hands dripped with perfume, my fingers*
> *with lovely myrrh, as I pulled back the bolt. I opened to my lover, but*
> *he was gone. I yearned even for his voice! I searched for him, but I*
> *couldn't find him anywhere.*
>
> (Song of Solomon 5:4–6)

God reckons that good sex is great!

The Bible celebrates the beauty of a man and a woman being joined through sexual love. Love is possibly the most explosive and powerful force in the universe and sex is an overflow from it. Sex has the power to unite two people and make them one. It has the potential to create new life and begin families. Because of this, sex needs to go hand in hand with commitment, faithfulness and love.

But the sad reality is that so many people experience sex without love and commitment. Instead of fulfilment, the story is of sexually transmitted infections, unfaithfulness, unwanted pregnancies, abortions, guilt, regret, relationships breaking up and families breaking down.

Many young people tell me that having sex wasn't all it was cracked up to be. They decided to have sex to fit in, to keep their partner happy, to prove they weren't gay, to find out if they *were* gay, or because they were drunk or curious or just didn't know how to say no. They thought it would bring them the love or security they were looking for. Often, they were left disappointed.

Sometimes sex can end up being a pretty messy business, and because what we do always affects other people, messy sex is bad news for all of us.

Girl on a Bench

I once heard a story that broke my heart.

A teenage girl was found sitting on a bench in a North London park at two in the morning. When asked what she was doing there she said she was waiting for someone. The 'someone' was a stranger, or a number of different strangers, who would come by and ask her for sex. She didn't get paid for it and later admitted that she didn't want to have sex this way; what she wanted was 'a cup of tea'.

Aged fourteen, this beautiful young girl was learning that sex without love, commitment, faithfulness, communication, security and kindness was empty. It was less exciting than a cup of tea.

Deal or No Deal?

I know that by now you will have had 'the sex talk' about how babies are made!

When I first learnt about sex I thought it was disgusting and no-one in their right minds would ever do it (I was very young at the time!). I went home from school and told my mum what I had heard in the playground and was horrified when she told me that not only is sex not disgusting, but that she and Dad did it – often!

As I grew up I realized that there are many different ideas about sex.

So let me ask you: what do you think about sex? What is it for? Who invented it? What makes sex OK or not OK?

One idea is that we are just animals so we should do what we want whenever we want. People who think this say that there isn't a right or a wrong way to have sex. You should just do what feels right to you.

But if sex is just an animal urge, then why do we (unlike animals) fall in love? And it's obvious that we can't have sex with anyone we want, whenever we want. This leads to the worst kind of sex and people who do this are called abusers or rapists. We have to agree that having sex with someone is about more than just satisfying an individual sexual urge. To make sure sex is good for everyone involved, it needs to happen in some kind of relationship in which the two people know they aren't being used or abused.

Another idea is that sex was created by a loving God who wants to give great gifts to his creation. All the mammals and animals that he made were able to reproduce to continue their species, but to human beings he gave the gift of sexual intimacy. This means the innermost part of one person intertwining with the innermost part of another person.

The Bible calls this 'becoming one flesh' – like one person. In fact, sex is so fantastic that people refer to it as 'knowing' each other or 'making love'. In

Ephesians chapter 5, Paul calls a loving, committed sexual relationship a 'profound mystery'.

God's gift of sex is always a good idea, but it is possible to experience it in the wrong way. To protect us from being hurt and hurting others through having sex the wrong way, God created the boundary of marriage. All God's boundaries are for our safety and our success. His boundary of saving sex for marriage is not to dampen our sexual enjoyment but to give us more of a chance of having it.

People who have different sexual partners can sometimes find it harder to go deeper emotionally with their partners because they fear being left hurting like last time. As sex is a physical, emotional and spiritual experience, we need to be free to give ourselves completely in sexual intimacy to our husband or wife.

Which idea about sex makes more sense?

Which idea do you think is better for everyone?

Phone-tastic!

Imagine you created a whole new type of phone that could transform itself into a hair straightener, stream high-definition videos straight from the Internet and tell you what people were thinking! You decide to be generous and give one of these phones to all your friends. At first they are really excited, but after a while you notice they are using it only to send messages and make calls. Whenever you try to remind them about everything else their phone can do, they tell you to stop interfering because they know what they are doing.

How would it make you feel?

How do you think God feels when his gift of sex is not being enjoyed to the full by people in the way he meant it to be? Can you imagine how disappointed he must be that we think he has nothing to say about the sex that he created?

The God Sex Guide

There is a book for adults called *The Good Sex Guide*.[2] I remember once sneaking into a bookshop to take a look at a copy! It was full of top tips for getting the most out of your sex life. As I stood flicking through the pages I suddenly realized how cold and calculated it all was. Surely having a good sex life is more about having a strong relationship than about knowing the best sexual techniques? Even the sexiest people in the world can have terrible relationships and unsatisfying sex.

Getting rid of bad sex has to start with understanding what good sex is.

Understanding what good sex is starts with listening to the creator of sex. So here are four 'Ps' that will help us understand God's guide to sex!

1. Procreation

The very first people on earth were created to live in a world that would care for them and which they could care for. It was an incredible life. They were close to God (the Bible says he walked with them), they were close to the world around them (Adam gave the animals names), and they were close to each other (they were naked but it didn't embarrass them). God placed them in an environment where they had everything they needed. They didn't get insect bites, sunburn or homework!

It was a perfect world.

God also gave them a job to do; they were to look after the world and fill it with more and more people who would also care for each other and the world God had made. This meant that they had to have sex – it was part of the job description!

> God blessed them and told them, 'Multiply and fill the earth and subdue it. Be masters over the fish and birds and all the animals.'
>
> (Genesis 1:28)

Adam and Eve quickly discovered that everything God made was good: trees, waterfalls, sunsets, fruit trees, work and sex. Just as Eve was created out of a bone from Adam's side, so making love brought them back together to be like one person again. Some people call it 'sexual union'. In many ways it is more like a sexual *reunion*. The Bible calls it 'one flesh'. When God created Eve, Adam exclaimed:

> 'At last! She is part of my own flesh and bone! She will be called "woman", for she was taken out of man.' This explains why a man leaves his father and mother and is joined to his wife, and the two are united into one.
>
> (Genesis 2:23–24)

When Adam and Eve had sex they knew total connection with each other. This sex connection was so strong in God's eyes that it required them to be exclusive and faithful, having sex with only one other person for ever.

People were to be faithful to that one person just as God was faithful to them. Having sex was never meant to be a series of one-off experiences shared with different people.

When Adam and Eve lost their virginity it wasn't on their wedding night, because they didn't get married. But the pattern of people committing themselves to each other and carrying on the human race through sex in loving, faithful and exclusive relationships had begun. Since the beginning people have got married (in different ways in different cultures) to show just how committed and exclusive their relationship is.

There is so much evidence around today that shows us just how right God got it! Children who are born into happy and stable families find it easier to feel confident in their abilities and potential. Children and adults who grow up not knowing one or both of their parents often feel they have missed out. It can be unbelievably difficult for a child growing up not knowing security at home. It was never meant to be like this.

2. Promise

How good are you at keeping promises?

Do people keep their promises to you?

One of the biggest promises anyone can make in their life is the commitment to 'love and honour' someone 'till death do us part'. Even though marriage has been around for years, it is still as popular today as it has ever been. Even young people who have been through the heartbreak of parental divorce often still want to get married. Why?

Forget the white dress and the reception on a luxury yacht for a minute. Marriage is simply a man and a woman saying to God and their friends that from now on they will be faithful to each other. This means they will promise to look for intimate sexual love and deep emotional support only from each other, even if someone 'better' comes along. This doesn't mean that they dump all their mates. They still need meaningful relationships with close friends and family, but they will give their heart and body as a complete whole only to each other.

What an incredible promise to make to someone.

Imagine you were walking down the corridor at school and the guy of your dreams came up to you and, in front of all your friends, took your hand, looked you in the eye and said, 'I have been waiting for you all my life. I love you and no-one else. I want to spend the rest of my life getting to know you.'

How would you feel?

You would be on cloud nine! You wouldn't be able to stop talking in class. You wouldn't be able to eat anything at lunch. You wouldn't be able to concentrate on anything.

Imagine that the next day you were walking down the same corridor when the guy of your dreams came up to you and your friends again. You get all excited about what he is going to say today. What could beat yesterday's outpouring of love and devotion?

He walks towards you and, in front of all your mates, he takes your best friend's hands, looks into her eyes and says, 'I have been waiting for you all my life. I love you and no-one else. I want to spend the rest of my life getting to know you.'

What?

You are devastated. Crushed. Angry. Confused. Heartbroken.

He had made that promise to *you*. How could he now say it to her?

When promises are broken, we can feel broken. God intended sex to be an overflow of love and commitment in a happy and faithful relationship. It is not a random act, but a sign of commitment, a promise that you are willing to give yourself intimately and exclusively to another person.

This is why the Bible is so keen that we understand the importance of saving sexual intimacy for the person we marry. In a letter Paul wrote to Christians in the first century, he talked about how important it is that Jesus' followers live differently from the rest of society to show just how incredible the life that Jesus offers is. Paul was passionately concerned that people who had been set free from lifestyles that were destroying them shouldn't go back to their old habits and patterns. In Hebrews he lists a load of things that Christians needed to be committed to doing in this new life they had been given: loving each other like a family, being kind and welcoming to strangers, visiting people in prison, being wise with their money and saving sex for marriage.

> *Keep on loving each other like brother and sisters. Do not forget to entertain strangers for by doing so some people have entertained*

> *angels without knowing it. Remember those in prison as if you*
> *were their fellow prisoners . . . Marriage should be honoured by all*
> *and the marriage bed kept pure, for God will judge the adulterer*
> *and all the sexually immoral. Keep your lives free from the love of*
> *money and be content with what you have, because God has said,*
> *'Never will I leave you, never will I forsake you.' So we say with con-*
> *fidence, 'The Lord is my helper, I will not be afraid. What can man do*
> *to me?'*

(Hebrews 13:1–6)

Having sex outside marriage is no 'worse' a sin than being selfish with your money or unkind to strangers. All these things can damage individuals and whole communities. God wants to be our helper in dealing with all these areas in our lives. He wants us to be good with our money, loving to people around us, passionate about injustice in our world and sexually pure, because this is the best way to live free and happy lives. What we do with our money as well as our bodies has consequences not only for us but also for the people around us – it all matters to God.

This is why sex matters to God. Because he made us and also made sex, there is always a spiritual thing (a God moment) going on when people have sex. Something happens between two people when they have sex, even if they are not in love.

If you have sex with someone (even if it is oral sex or just touching each other's body in a sexual way), you are making a powerful connection with them. Being casual about what you do with your body means that you are being casual about how people are treating your heart. Your heart, spirit and body are very precious, so protect them.

You are like a private garden, my treasure, my bride. You are like a spring that no-one else can drink from, a fountain of my own.

(Song of Solomon 4:12)

3. Protection

Most films tell the story of a hero who overcomes all the odds to rescue the heroine. There are some exceptions to this rule, but on the whole the guy ends up protecting the girl and saving the day. Generally, most boys like protecting girls. They like to be a shoulder for girls to cry on. They want girls to see them as strong and manly. They might be a bad brother but they still have a go at anyone else who gives their sister a hard time!

It's really great to have guys like this around. But it's also true that we can do a lot to protect ourselves and each other. If you want to get good at protecting your heart and body, you need to get good at thinking for yourself. It is really important to know a few of the facts about the consequences of sex.

Pregnancy
The first consequence of sex that people think about is pregnancy.

It is a fact that teenage girls are often at the peak of their fertility, which means that it can be very easy for them to become pregnant. I meet girls who say they had sex only once and became pregnant – this isn't unusual. The biological purpose of sex is to reproduce, so during sex your body will do all it can to make sure that the sperm reaches and fertilizes the egg. Sticking your head in the sand and hoping that it won't happen to you won't stop biology from working!

I met a young couple who found out they were pregnant and didn't know what to do. They felt that they couldn't tell anyone, not even their parents. In the end they opted for an abortion. But it was more difficult to have an abortion than they thought. For weeks afterwards they both felt strange towards each other and guilty about what they had done. Eventually they ended their relationship and went on to meet other people, hurt and full of regrets. Even though they were very young, both of them wished they had made a different decision – not only about the abortion, but also about having sex in the first place.

STIs
Sexually transmitted infections (STIs) are infections that are passed from one person to another during sexual activity through body fluids (such as blood), via secretions from the vagina or penis, or through genital contact. There are many STIs around. Some, such as chlamydia and gonorrhoea, are bacterial and are passed when a couple have sexual intercourse (including oral sex). They can be cleared up by a course of antibiotics from a doctor. As many people who contract chlamydia or gonorrhoea don't have any symptoms, they don't think anything is wrong and they don't get to the clinic to be treated.

A close friend of mine contracted chlamydia when we were both fifteen, through having sex with a boy she met at a party. She was so worried about getting pregnant that when her period started she was so relieved that she didn't even think there might be something harmful in her body that would lie undetected like a dark secret for many years. Eventually, after years of trying with her husband for a baby, she discovered that the chlamydia infection in her body had made her infertile and she would never be able to have a baby.

Other STIs are viral, which means that once someone has contracted one they can never be rid of it. A viral STI that you will have heard of is HIV, which becomes AIDS. People who are HIV positive will never be able to get rid of the virus from their body, and over the years the virus will destroy their immune system. Unless we find a cure they will eventually die of AIDS, because their immune system has become so weak that even a common cold or flu is fatal to them.

Genital warts are a less-well-known viral STI. Lara slept with her boyfriend when they had been going out for seven months. They both felt ready for sex but were still too shy and insecure to talk about the consequences. Lara was a virgin and knew that Ben had been with girls before. But they had sex anyway, and then they broke up. Two weeks after they had split up, Lara came to me with a very embarrassing problem: she had a very itchy vagina and there were red sores around it. We went to see the nurse at the clinic, who told Lara that, even though her boyfriend had used a condom, he had still given her genital warts. Lara will never be rid of the virus in her body, but she will be able to keep it under control with treatment from the clinic. The itching has stopped but she knows that the sores could reappear at any time. Lara feels really ashamed of having genital warts and knows that when she falls in love and wants to build a new life with someone, she will have to tell them about her STI.

Our bodies aren't built to cope with sexual promiscuity. Not having sex or having sex with only one person all your life, who doesn't have an STI, are the only two ways to be 100% sure that you will never get an STI.

Saving sex for marriage is not only the best idea for your heart and emotions, it is also one of the best things you can do to avoid STIs and increase your chances of having babies in the future.

Having sex changes everything: feelings, self-esteem, confidence, options, relationships and the future.

Using condoms properly during sexual intercourse lowers the chance of a pregnancy or passing on STIs, but it doesn't take away the possibility altogether – they are not magic! Some STIs (such as genital warts, pubic lice and genital herpes) can be passed through people merely touching each other's genital area.

The question you need to ask yourself is whether having sex with someone before you are married to them is worth the risk of maybe getting pregnant or contracting an STI.

Is it worth risking your physical and emotional health for a moment with someone you may not be with for the rest of your life?

It is possible to have sex with lots of different people – but it isn't good for our body, let alone our mind and heart. Saving sex for marriage or not having sex again until you get married makes the best sense.

4. Possibility

Place me like a seal over your heart, or like a seal on your arm. For love is as strong as death, and its jealousy as unyielding as the grave. Love flashes like fire, the brightest kind of flame. Many waters cannot quench love; neither can rivers drown it. If a man tried

> *to buy love with everything he owned, his offer would be utterly*
> *despised.*
>
> (Song of Solomon 8:6)

One of the greatest gifts that God has given us is the ability to create new life.

Every time a man and a woman have sex until the woman reaches menopause, there is the possibility for that miracle to occur. Contraception (such as using a condom or being on the pill) can reduce the possibility of conception (getting pregnant), but it can never totally eliminate it.

Sex also gives us the possibility of experiencing completeness in a way that makes both partners feel loved, secure, trusted and whole. Sex isn't the road to this kind of happiness, but in a marriage built on trust, respect and commitment, sex gives you both one of the most exciting and powerful ways of relating to each other.

As sexual intimacy is a gift from God, it is possible to have sex in such a way that it gives glory to him! Saving sex for marriage is a way of putting God and his purposes first in your life and relationship.

More to Life Than Sex

The life that God has given us is not just about having sex!

It's also not about always having a boyfriend. Living fully for God might mean having a boyfriend or husband, but it also might mean being single for a while. There are some people who stay single all their lives, and find deep and fulfilling relationships with close friends.

God wants you to be cherished in all your friendships and relationships and he created you to be able to love in return. Because of the way that you have been loved by people in your life, you will respond to love in different ways. For some of you, the challenge is to let people love you and treat you well. For others of you, it might mean making tough decisions about the relationships you are in. You might want people to believe that everything is OK when in fact you are struggling to cope with a controlling boyfriend or feelings of guilt about having sex.

It's not always easy to live God's way. Every day we are with people who think very differently about sex and relationships. I believe that doing this God's way will help us know sexual intimacy in the best way possible.

> *Being a Christian is much more complicated than praying one prayer. The decisions we make about how we show love to our boyfriends and how we use our bodies say a lot about how we understand living with God every day. We need to remember that God's forgiveness is much bigger than any mistakes we might make. And when we bring our mistakes to Jesus he will forgive and forget them even if we struggle to. It doesn't stop there – he will walk with us every day, helping us to use our bodies and hearts in holy and brilliant ways.*
>
> (Katy)

Wonder_land

- What do you think about God's plan that sexual intimacy should be saved for marriage? Do you think it is possible to wait for marriage before you have sex?
- Some people say that, as long as you love someone, it doesn't matter if you don't wait to get married to them before you have sex. If sex is about becoming 'one flesh' with someone, is it wise to do this before you are married?
- 'If you are not ready to have a baby or deal with an STI, you're not ready to have sex.' What do you think about this statement?
- There is no verse in the Bible that actually says 'don't have sex before marriage'. There are many verses that encouraged the early Christians not to get involved in 'sexual immorality'. The Greek word *pornea* (translated into English as 'sexual immorality') meant any sexual activity outside marriage: adultery, sex before marriage, abuse, rape, etc. Look up these verses where the word *pornea* is used: 1 Corinthians 6:18; Ephesians 5:3–4; Colossians 3:5–6; 1 Thessalonians 4:3–5; Hebrews 12:16; 1 Peter 4:3.
- What qualities do you look for in someone you are going out with?
- How important is it to you that they share your values when it comes to sex?
- Do you know a couple who have been married for a while? Why not ask them what has helped them remain faithful and loving in their marriage.

My Sanctuary

Sit down somewhere comfy and take a few deep breaths. I have thrown a load of ideas at you in this chapter and you probably feel a bit overwhelmed – that's OK. Now is your chance to allow the chapter to settle into your heart.

As you think back over the chapter, which words or ideas stand out for you? What questions do you have? Write them down in the space below.

It is really important that you chat through your questions with a wise woman. Don't leave them here on the page. Your questions matter because the way you deal with sexual temptations will affect your future life and relationships, so don't be shy. You are not alone in what you are thinking and feeling.

If you can, put on some chill-out music and read the verse from the Song of Solomon below. Why not memorize it and repeat it to yourself (in your head!) during the day. You are God's treasured daughter, and that truth lives in you like a beautiful secret. Your sexuality is precious to him and precious to you. Treasure It, and don't just give away your kisses and heart to any guy who asks!

> *You are like a private garden, my treasure, my bride. You are like a spring that no-one else can drink from, a fountain of my own.*
>
> (Song of Solomon 4:12)

Chapter Eight
What Are You Waiting For?

Café Romance

As I write this in a coffee shop in Harrow, I can see through the window a teenage couple sitting on a bench, engrossed in each other. He must have said something gorgeous to her because she has just thrown her arms around him with a huge smile on her face. Right now, in this moment, no-one and nothing else in the world exists for them.

They look great.

They look happy.

When they are together, what are they hoping for?

When they are apart, what are they waiting for?

She is chatting away at him and he is reaching for his phone. To get his attention focused back onto her she kisses him, and although he gives in for the first few kisses he soon realizes there are other people around and pulls away, embarrassed. She flashes him a hurt look and sulks. He takes her hand and then I look up again and the bench is empty; they have gone.

It makes me think of all the thousands and millions of relationships and kisses that are happening at this very moment.

I have sat in that same coffee shop often since then but I have never seen that young couple again. I hope that they are still together, getting to know each other better, breaking up and making up, building a future together. I imagine them older, with kids and a mortgage. I imagine them with grandchildren and hearts full of memories.

Being with someone is a big deal. All sorts of things can happen as a result of having a boyfriend: falling in love, getting your heart broken, getting engaged, getting married, having kids and grandkids!

Because of this, Christians can feel a lot of confusion about dating and just what saving sex for marriage means. Is it OK to go out with someone? Is it OK to kiss your boyfriend? What about holding hands?

By far the most frequent question that young Christians ask me is, 'How far is too far?'

Have you ever asked that question? Have you ever thought about why you ask that question?

I think that deep down we all realize that there are limits to how far we should go in a relationship. Maybe we have been taught that sex should be saved for marriage – but we don't know why. Or we have been hurt before and don't want to be vulnerable again. Whatever the reason, we all know that relationships are costly and shouldn't be treated lightly.

So, how far is too far?

Most young couples who ask me this question are in fact asking the question, 'How much sexual stuff can we get away with before annoying God or getting caught out?'

It's great to ask questions, but the problem with this one is that it is the wrong question to ask.

Relationships get stronger by growing in intimacy.

Intimacy doesn't mean having sex; it means learning to trust each other emotionally (this person cherishes your thoughts and feelings), spiritually (this person helps you love Jesus more), and physically (this person treats you with respect and affection).

For a relationship to work, intimacy in all these areas needs to grow at the same time. This is why something that begins as a fling or a one-night stand very rarely grows into a strong and trusting relationship. It also means that young Christians who go out with each other should find ways of showing love and affection to each other physically. The difficulty is in knowing how much physical affection it is OK to show to someone before you are married to them!

Take a look at the following list, and ask yourself how comfortable you would be sharing that experience with a boyfriend and how it might affect your relationship. (The list is not written in order of how things should happen!)

- Holding hands
- Cuddling on a couch or bed in front of the TV
- Walking arm in arm

- Praying together
- Spending most of your time together in one of your bedrooms
- Touching each other with clothes still on
- Touching inside clothes
- Chatting about faith together
- Inviting your boyfriend round to meet your family
- Having a long kiss
- Having sex
- Going out on a date
- Sleeping in the same bed together
- Sharing your secret hopes and dreams with each other
- Hugging each other
- Going on holiday with your boyfriend and his family
- Being naked together and touching each other
- Chatting for ages on the phone to each other
- Spending every spare moment together.

How did you get on?

Did you find you could decide on what sort of things you would feel comfortable with in a relationship?

Do you think it is possible to feel comfortable with things you shouldn't be doing?

Why not take this list to an older friend you trust and see what they think about the boundaries you have set yourself. If you are already in a relationship, talk to your boyfriend about where you both will set your boundaries. It is a good idea for you both to find someone you feel happy to talk to about your boundaries, because there will be times when you will find it difficult to stick to them.

It can be so embarrassing to talk about these things with your boyfriend, but if you are going out with someone then you need to get used to doing so. Some young couples think that if they don't talk about sex then they won't get tempted. This never works, and you are more likely to end up in a situation you know is wrong if you don't talk at the start about your boundaries and how to be accountable.

If I were to ask you what you think is crucial in any relationship, I am sure that you would say words such as 'trust, respect, communication and love'. Talking with your boyfriend about how far you will go physically is a really good way of testing whether you are with someone who respects and loves you. If they won't respect your values they don't respect *you*, and, as painful as this sounds, you are better off without them. Love isn't a fuzzy feeling; it is a decision to put the other person's needs and values before your own.

The Bible teaches us that our actions should always be motivated by love. This doesn't just affect the way we treat the lonely girl in the corner of the class; it also affects how we treat our boyfriends or potential boyfriends.

Loving your boyfriend means helping him stick to your agreed boundaries. Being loved in return means that you never feel pressured into doing something to keep him happy or to stop him from leaving you.

Before I was married I decided that I was happy to go out with boyfriends but I wanted to save really sexually intimate things for my husband. I didn't want to get naked, sleep in a bed with a guy, touch his naked body or have sex with anyone until I married him. Most of the time I kept to these boundaries, but sometimes I went further than planned. Even though I was a virgin when I got married, I remember feeling a lot of guilt and regret when I went further physically than I wanted to. I didn't know whom to talk to about everything that was going on in my head, so I found that I quickly did the same things again and again.

All of us get 'turned on' (sexually aroused) by certain things. You need to know what turns you on, because, once you are in the throes of passion, it's really hard to engage your brain! Knowing what turns you both on can help you learn when you need to stop and do something different together. Even though it can feel really exciting turning each other on, it can quickly lead to your feeling guilty and resentful, which isn't exciting at all.

One way to deal with temptation in a relationship is to be honest about your struggles and to find other ways of showing love and affection. You also need to forgive each other when you go further than planned. This way you can discover so much about each other and why God's idea of saving sex for marriage is such a good, although tough, one.

Through not having sex before you get married, you have a way of proving to each other that you have self-control and can be trusted to be faithful.

I sometimes get asked if it's OK to go out with someone if you aren't serious about getting married to them. It's worth remembering that there's a difference between being serious about marriage and being serious about having a good relationship. The reality is that the person you go out with when you are 14 is probably not going to be the person you marry when you are older. But even if marriage isn't your main priority in a relationship when you are young, you need to realise that it is probably where you are heading if you want to have sex one day and a family. This doesn't mean that it is bad to date someone when you are young, but it means you need to be very wise about what that relationship is like. The most important ingredients of your relationship should be kindness, respect and integrity. If you do want to marry when you are older, think about the things you may regret having done with previous boyfriends. That is a good place to start to draw the line now.

Obsession

I would like to throw in a couple of notes of caution here.

The first is that sometimes people can get really obsessed with not having sex.

In trying to stay sexually pure, it can be very easy to fall into the trap of thinking that all thoughts and feelings about sex are wrong and dirty. This isn't true.

Sex is good. It is to be enjoyed. Waiting for it is part of the enjoyment, even though it can be a really difficult thing to do.

The reason for having boundaries that you both agree to is to free you to build a loving and healthy relationship founded on trust, not sex. Sex is such a powerful experience that if you get too physical too quickly with someone it is almost impossible to go back and build in the other more important things, such as trust, respect and love. Choosing not to spend every spare moment together is just as important as not getting naked together, as both these things can put too much pressure on a relationship.

The second note of caution is about falling in love.

When you fall in love with someone it feels like your whole world has changed. When you are with them you dread the time you will have to part and when you are apart you count every second until you meet again! We feel that all we need in life is to be with them and that nothing bad can touch us. But have you also noticed that there is a difference between being in love with someone and being infatuated with them? Infatuation is an intense, powerful and sometimes controlling feeling. When we are infatuated with someone we get obsessed about where they are or who they are talking to. We want them to make us feel good all the time and when they let us down (which they will, because they are only human) we feel devastated and abandoned.

Time for a reality check.

Only God can fully satisfy us and fill the longing in our hearts.

Being obsessed about a guy or being obsessed about not having sex can both lead us away from finding our true identity and worth in God. Falling in love and having sex in a happy marriage are great gifts from God to wait for and treasure.

> *I want you to promise, O women of Jerusalem, not to awaken love until the time is right.*

> (Song of Solomon 8:4)

As well as choosing to save sex as something to explore with my husband, I had to realize that God chose to forgive me every time I turned to him. He promised to give me the strength to be strong and faithful.

Saying no is hard. It's particularly hard when you say no to a guy you really love and who really loves you.

The focus on waiting for sex is not so that sex will be perfect when you get married. The purpose of waiting is so that you can build up a really strong foundation of trust, love and faithfulness – this is the glue that holds marriages together. Sex isn't the be-all and end-all of a marriage, but a marriage built on loving and intimate friendship has the potential to last.

Heartache

How can a young person live a clean life?
By carefully reading the map of your Word.
I'm single-minded in pursuit of you;
Don't let me miss the road signs you've posted.
(Psalm 119:9, *The Message*)

God wants so much for us. He's the best dad there is. He longs for us to have relationships with people who will help us grow as followers of Jesus as well as with people who don't know him. He knows how easy it can be to start building unhealthy patterns that can trap us in behaviour that isn't godly or good for us.

I meet girls who sleep with Christians guys because they trust that if the guy says having sex is OK, it must be. After all, he's a Christian, so he must be right. Right?

I know girls who have real heartaches over the fact that they have non-Christian boyfriends. They may have been praying and praying for a boyfriend and then someone comes along but he's not a Christian, so they pray and pray and fall more and more in love with him and think that maybe, just maybe, if they hold on long enough he might find Jesus.

I sometimes wonder if focusing on trying to 'convert' their boyfriend has meant that some of them have failed to see what their relationship is actually like. A non-Christian lad isn't a bad person, but he probably won't be able to help you go further in your relationship with Jesus. It's not your job to change him to make him boyfriend material or even Christian boyfriend material. Your job is to grow in your relationship with God. Ending a relationship is always painful. God asks that you speak with him about your questions and trust that he will heal your heart and guide you in future relationships.

I know young couples who spend all their time trying not to have sex but are desperate to go a little bit further each time. Turning each other on and then pulling back becomes addictive. They fail to see that, without that cycle of excitement and guilt, they might not have a relationship at all.

Or maybe you know girls who have a number of different boyfriends. They get physical with one boyfriend and then that relationship ends so they go out with someone else. But to feel as close to this new boyfriend as to their last one they need to go as far with them as they did with the last guy and even further, so that they feel closer to this new person. And then this relationship ends and they go out with yet another guy and they need to go as far with this guy as they did with the other two lads, and even further.

When does the cycle stop? When do we face what's really happening and take control of what we are doing? Have you ever been so involved in a relationship (your own or a friend's) that you have forgotten that:

- Christian boys won't automatically make great boyfriends – you both need to work at the relationship and set honest and helpful boundaries?
- Non-Christian boys won't automatically come to know Jesus if you go out with them?

Being a Christian won't protect you from having to deal with temptation or getting your fingers burnt or ending up heartbroken.

But when it comes to matters of the heart you are in safe hands. The God who made your heart knows your desires. He also knows that there is a limit to your powers! No matter how much we might long to see our friends or boyfriends come to know God, changing is between them and him.

Wait Well

Waiting for what you are longing for is a bit of a theme in human life. This is because anything worth having is worth waiting for.

Let's say you had arranged to meet a friend on a Saturday to go shopping together. You catch the bus from home but there is so much traffic and roadworks that you end up being really late to meet them. How long would you want them to wait for you? If they waited for only a few minutes before they went home, what would that tell you about how they felt about you? If, however, when you eventually turned up two hours late you found them sitting on the bench, patiently waiting for you, how would that make you feel?

Waiting is good.

Even though your friend was sitting doing nothing while they waited for you, this nothingness was everything! It was telling you that you are very important to them. It was also telling you that they were the kind of friend worth having: patient, faithful, kind. This experience would strengthen your friendship in a way that no amount of presents and good times together could do.

What about waiting for sex?

Could *not* having sex with your boyfriend actually make your relationship with him deeper?

Could waiting for sex until you get married actually make your marriage stronger?

Could not having sex now, even if you don't know whether you will ever get married, make you more convinced that there is much more to life than sex?

These are big questions, and even if you aren't facing them yet, you will one day! Saving sex for marriage doesn't mean that it will be mind-blowingly awesome the first time you have it. But it does mean that you will have concentrated on building a relationship based on trust and faithfulness even before you ever have sex. That is the best start to any sexual relationship.

Wonder_land

Take a look at Lauren's story below.

> *I had never dated anyone until I met this young man. It was just wonderful . . . We were getting to know each other's hearts, where we were going in life and what our dreams were. We didn't hold hands. We decided early on that we didn't want to do that, we didn't want to add any physical touch because we felt that would be distracting from getting to know the heart of the other person.*
>
> (Lauren Wilson,
> from *The Virgin Daughters*, Channel 4)[1]

- Lauren decided not to date any boy until she met someone she was going to marry. What do you think about her choice? What might be some of the benefits and disadvantages of this approach to dating?
- How do people know that they are ready to start going out on dates?
- How can you make sure that you don't waste your teenage years in a wrong relationship or obsessing after Mr Right?
- How much time and energy do you spend thinking about boyfriends and relationships?

- If you are starting a new relationship, how can you make sure that you both feel comfortable and confident with your physical and emotional boundaries?
- If you are already in a relationship, what can you both do to make the relationship stronger and put clearer boundaries around your physical and emotional intimacy? Why not write a list of 101 things you are going to enjoy doing together, like speaking for hours on the phone, writing each other letters, holding hands on long walks, sharing your most embarrassing moment, planning mystery dates and winking at each other across a crowded room!

My Sanctuary

Think about the last thing you had to wait for.

What were you like at waiting for it?

Did you wait patiently or did you jump around, annoyed that you had to wait so long?

The times when I struggle with waiting for something I want are when I think that I have been forgotten – such as in a café or waiting for someone to give me a lift home. I don't have a lot of faith that what I am waiting for will finally happen.

Waiting well has a lot to do with having faith.

Having faith in God, even in the most difficult situations, can help us to wait patiently for the good gifts we know he will give us. It might be the gift of someone we fall in love with and marry. It might be the gift of a close friend when we feel so lonely, or a job that we really want. The most important good gift that God gives us is the chance to know him more closely. The Bible says that people can see that your faith is in God by the way you act in different situations – by the way you display the 'fruits of the Spirit' that we read about earlier. Imagine you have a cup full of hot chocolate and someone bumps into you. What comes out of the cup? Hot chocolate.

What is inside comes out.

It's the same with us. People can't see what kind of a person we really are on the inside until someone happens to knock it out of us! If we are full of anger, then we are quick to shout or blame other people when we get hurt. If we are full of despair, then we are quick to sort things out for ourselves rather than wait for God to show us what to do. If we are full of love and faith that God cares for us, then we can show patience even in the most difficult times.

> *For when your faith is tested, your endurance has a chance to grow. So let it grow, for when your endurance is fully developed, you will be strong in character and ready for anything. If you need wisdom – if you want to know what God wants you to do – ask him, he will gladly tell you.*
>
> (James 1:5)

Why not switch your phone off and spend time listening to God? Write down any words or pictures that come into your mind.

What is God asking you to wait for?

As you wait, what are you learning about yourself?

What is God teaching you about himself?

If you are unsure what God has said to you, share it with an older Christian and ask them to listen to God with you.

Chapter Nine
Nice Guys

Each girl was given a Post-it note to write a question on. It was an all-girl workshop and we had spent most of the afternoon talking about friends, boys and the latest thing on TV. As the Post-it notes came back I was amazed to see that, entirely independently, each girl had written pretty much the same question. It was this: 'I like this guy – how do I know if he likes me?'

I looked around the room. Even the girls I thought would be more interested in maths than in boys were still perplexed by that age-old question. Our mothers and grandmothers would have asked it. The woman walking down the street, the lady serving up the school dinner and the girl catching the bus with us probably all want to know the same thing. And it's this:

> How do I know if he likes me?
> How do I know if he is the one for me?
> How will I accept it if he doesn't like me?

But we aren't alone. It's not just girls who are asking these questions – boys are asking the same things too.

> How do I know if she likes me?
> How do I know if she is the one for me?
> How will I accept it if she doesn't like me?

Boy World

There is a scene in the film *Enchanted*[1] in which Princess Gisele, recently freed from a cartoon existence, goes on a shopping spree with Morgan, the daughter of the guy she has fallen in love with. They end up in a hair salon and their conversation turns to boys.

'And when you go out you don't want to wear too much make-up, cos otherwise the boys get the wrong idea and you know how they are. They're only after one thing,' Morgan informs Gisele.

'What's that?' asks Gisele.

'I don't know,' Morgan replies with a smile. 'No-one will tell me.'

There is a widely held belief that boys are after only one thing, and that one thing is sex! But is this really true, and is it fair to boys? Are there some guys out there who value girls as friends and want a relationship in which they can be themselves and feel cared for?

> What do lads want?
> What's going on in a guy's heart and brain?

I can hear your answers:

> *'Nothing!'*
> *'What, guys have brains?!'*
> *'I don't think that guys know what's going on in their heads – so how on earth are we supposed to know?'*

OK, before we sink any further, let's take a closer look at the lads. During puberty, teenage boys are discovering new things about themselves. Their bodies are changing and producing loads of testosterone, which means they want to take risks and prove themselves. They want to stand out from the crowd either through physical strength (being the best at sports, or fighting) or through humour (being the joker in the group). Boys who don't manage to stand out from the crowd in these ways can experience a lot of nervousness, particularly around girls.

Teenage boys also have to go through the embarrassment of their voices dropping (becoming deeper), learning how to shave (without cutting themselves), dealing with spots and getting erections (blood rushing to the penis, making it hard). During their teenage years boys are coming to terms with their sudden and urgent interest in sex and girls, and this can be confusing for even the most confident-looking lad.

It is true that boys (like girls) are curious about sex and the opposite sex.

It is true that boys (like girls) want to be attractive to others.

It is true that boys (like girls) are looking for someone they can be real with.

But boys also quickly realize that girls tend to go for the louder, more confident or funny lads. It might be easier to become friends with girls if you aren't loud, rude, dangerous or funny, but it's harder to get them to fancy you.

Are they right?

Are girls more attracted to 'dangerous' boys who are a bit arrogant and treat them badly?

Do the 'nice guys' always end up last in the race for a girl's attention?

Well, it depends on what we mean by 'bad lads' and 'nice guys'.

'Nice guys' are kind to kittens, help old grannies across the road and do your homework for you. 'Bad lads' brag about the number of girls they have got off with, regularly beat up the school nerd and pimp up their cars with alloys and a sound system!

If only it were as simple as that. The fact is that you can't always tell what a guy is like just by looking at him. If you really want to know what he is like, you need to get to know him. He might be one thing around his mates and quite another when he is just with you. Boys often feel under pressure to act in certain ways to impress the guys as well as the girls.

The best way to start a relationship with a boy is to become friends with him. Find out what he is into. Spend time with him in a larger group of friends as well as finding ways to chat with him on his own. This way, you know whether he is putting on an act and who he really is. Even if you meet on holiday and like each other from the start, you don't need to rush into a serious relationship straight away. The guy who is worthy of you will respect you all the more if you take your time in getting to know him. It will either make your relationship stronger or help you to realize that behind the cute smile this lad has none of the qualities you are interested in.

I don't know how you and your friends ask boys out. Do you send a 'messenger' to check out whether he is interested in you and report back? Sometimes this can work (and, let's face it, there is nothing more humiliating than asking a boy out and him saying 'no thanks'!) but sometimes it backfires badly.

The Magnet Effect

Bethany really liked Kieran and Kieran (unknown to Bethany) really liked Bethany.

Bethany didn't know how to tell him and didn't want to ruin their relationship by asking him out, so she agreed to her friend 'spying' for her. In true girl style, Bethany's friend approached Kieran in the school canteen and in front of a load of people asked him if he liked Bethany. More people gathered round to hear what was going on. Kieran felt backed into a corner and under pressure, so he said he didn't like Bethany, and stormed off. He ignored Bethany for the rest of the term. Bethany heard what he had said and ignored Kieran for the rest of the term.

They lost their friendship and any chance of dating, all because they couldn't be honest with each other about how they really felt.

It is the hardest thing in the world to let someone know you like them. You feel sick to your stomach and don't know what to do. Your greatest fear is that they will say they aren't interested in you and everyone will find out.

When people are attracted to each other they often act differently around each other. Some of the clues that a boy is interested in you might include:

- You catch him looking at you then quickly looking away when you see him.
- He finds any excuse to be near you even if he doesn't talk to you.
- He seems confused and a bit embarrassed around you.
- He runs off with something of yours to get you to chase after him!
- He shows off around you to impress you.
- He goes painfully silent around you.
- He spends ages on the phone or Internet chatting to you.
- You notice that he makes more of an effort with his appearance than before.
- None of the above!

Boys look for clues from the girls too to see if they are interested in them. If you do any of the following around a lad, he might think you are interested in him:

- If you single him out to talk to.
- If you text or call him for no reason.
- If you hug him lots or sit on his lap.
- If you have a lot of flesh on display (low-cut tops or tight clothing).
- If you look into his eyes when he is talking and laugh a lot at what he says.
- If you smile at him across the room.

The problem is that many girls do these things to guys they aren't attracted to. This is why things can get so confusing. Working out whether someone likes you isn't an exact science. To help the boys feel not quite so confused you need to check that the way you act around them doesn't send out the wrong signals. Sitting on a guy's lap might feel 'just friendly' to you, but for him it means much more. Having your body so close to him (and this includes long hugs) can really get a boy excited. The guys will misread the signals and think you want more.

Why Do Boys Do That?

Boys can be very confusing. Here is a collection of some of the crazy things lads get up to and a bit of insight into why they do it!

GIRL QUERY: 'My boyfriend Tom is really cuddly with me in private. He always holds my hand when we go out as just the two of us. But when we are out with his mates he pretty much ignores me. He always says sorry the next day, but why does he do it?' – Kate

BOY INSIGHT: 'Tom just wants to look macho in front of his mates. There's still an old saying among blokes, "Treat them mean to keep them keen." It means that you like to keep a girl confused about whether you like her or not because it makes her more dependent on you. It's a stupid saying, but if Tom is acting differently with you when he is with his friends then maybe he feels a bit insecure about your relationship. Instead of moaning at him about it, just let him know how much you like being with him. If he knows you are proud to be with him, it might help him feel more confident with you in front of his friends' – Jason

GIRL QUERY: 'There is this group of boys at school who always go round together and shout at the girls. It's really immature, and sometimes they say rude things to me and my friends. Why do they do that?' – Rhianne

BOY INSIGHT: 'If you think about it, girls go round in large groups too and boys find this really intimidating. These boys probably fancy you and your friends but because you are always together they need to feel stronger by having their crew around them. If you like one of the boys then you need to let him know that he can come and talk to you on his own. If you want them to stop then you need to ignore them. If you shout back at them they will keep going because, although you don't like them, they like the attention from you' – Mark

GIRL QUERY: 'Boys talk about sex all the time. Is it all they think of? Why do they get erections and then brag about them? It's weird' – Gemma

BOY INSIGHT: 'When boys are teenagers, anything can make them have an erection! Boys brag about it because they aren't as good as girls at talking about things that are happening to them. Most boys are pretty freaked out by it but also want to look like a player to their mates. It makes them feel like a man. If you want to help boys to think about more than just sex when they are around you, then wear clothes that leave more to the imagination. Seeing girls' breasts or cleavage is a major turn-on' – Ben

'No, it's not true – the world doesn't revolve around sex for us. When I chat with my friends we do talk about if a girl is sexy or not, but we mostly crack up about school and talk about relationships. Even the rude boys I know don't just want to talk about sex. Girls always say we only think about sex but we don't!' – André

GIRL QUERY: 'Whenever I try to talk to my boyfriend about things he always says he is too busy and has to go and meet someone. Why does he do that?' – Keira

BOY INSIGHT: 'Your boyfriend is probably scared that you want to try and change him. Girls find it so easy to talk about their emotions, but most boys find it really hard. The worst thing in any relationship is having to change who you are to be liked. If you want him to stay and chat, maybe write him a letter about how great you think he is and why you like being with him. I don't know what you want to talk to him about. Check your own motives first' – Martin

'In all honesty, a guy doesn't normally want to ask a girl about her problems because it leads to a fifteen-hour conversation! He is forced to sit and listen when all he wants to do is play on his X-Box. If a girl really wants to chat with her boyfriend about something important then she should wait until they are together and not call him up just for a big chat. Late-night chats on the phone might be great for girls but they make boys fall asleep!' – Mauro

Good Advice

I wonder how much time and energy you spend thinking about love, relationships and boys.

It's natural to want to share your life with someone, but wanting something too much can make you appear a bit desperate to the opposite sex. You are more likely to find someone you want to be with when you are least expecting it. Being yourself and letting people see who you are is the most attractive thing you can do.

Going out with someone is all about finding out more about him and yourself. You are both asking, 'Who are you and who am I?' There will be times when you want to be together on your own and times when you want to be together in a group of friends. It is always important to remember that in getting to know each other you might not like what you see (e.g. you might not share values), so it is OK to end the relationship. This can be a really sad and difficult thing to do, but it isn't the end of the world. The younger you are, the shorter your relationship with a boy will be. This is very normal, because you are on a huge learning curve and will change a whole lot before you become an adult and meet someone you want to be with for life. I am not saying that having loads of boyfriends is a good idea! But don't expect that the guy you start seeing when you are thirteen is still going to be the lad you want to marry when you are twenty-five.

The moment you have sex with someone the focus changes from the question 'Who are you and who am I?' to the statement 'You belong to me'. It can be terribly painful to end a sexual relationship because the break-up is a physical, emotional and spiritual separation. Both boys and girls feel huge emotions such as jealousy, envy, guilt and rejection because the person they became one with is not one with them any more.

Before you begin a relationship with a boy it is really helpful to ask God and friends you trust about whether they think this is a good relationship for you to be in. If you are longing to meet your future husband, you could convince yourself that the boy giving you a bit of attention is the one you have been waiting for. Longing for love and attention could mean that you are anyone's for the taking. The Bible encourages you to protect your heart above everything else. Why? Because your emotions and desires flow out of your heart and, if unchecked, can lead you to finding love in the wrong places or from people who can't love you as you should be loved.

Your heavenly Father invites you to trust him in everything. He knows your heart's desires.

Wonder_land

- Are you sometimes guilty of playing hard to get? Why do you do this? Has it ever ended well?
- Have you or your friends gone to the other extreme and 'pursued' the boys? Some girls can think that all boys are interested in is sex and so they are easy to get, or put pressure on boys to have sex with them. What do you think is the right way to treat boys?
- Why do some girls chase after the 'bad lads'? Could it be that girls think they can tame the lads or think that by being with them they will look more popular and valuable? What do you think?
- Make a list of the wrong reasons for going out with someone. What do you think are the right reasons for going out with someone?
- What things really frustrate you about boys? What things do you really appreciate about boys?
- Have you noticed your attitude to boys changing over time? Younger girls (aged ten to thirteen) are very interested in a boy's looks and style. As you get older, have you noticed that, although you still like a guy for his looks, you are more interested in his personality and qualities? This is very natural and part of growing up and understanding how relationships work. Women who are interested in a guy only for his looks tend to have more shallow and short-lived relationships that go nowhere.
- If you could tell all the boys in the world five things that they should know about girls, what would they be?

- If you could tell all the boys in the world five things you appreciate about them, what would they be?

My Sanctuary

What do you think about boys?

For a moment, step back from thinking of them as potential boyfriends!

How do you see boys?

> *When God made human beings, he chose to make two very different designs: male and female. Somehow, together, men and women express God's image. Then God said, 'Let us make humans in our image, to be like ourselves . . . ' So God created people in his own image; God patterned them after himself; male and female he created them.*
>
> (Genesis 1:26–27)

We live in a world that can be pretty down on guys most of the time. They can be blamed for being too macho one minute and too girly the next! God's plan is that guys and girls work together as a team to care for the world, bring about peace and justice and create new life, and, through doing these things, reflect his image. We may have different roles (especially in things such as childbirth), but we are equally loved and called by God.

Ask yourself what the guys in your life teach you about God's character.

When Paul wrote to the Christians in Ephesus he challenged them to live together in peace. Think about the ways that men and women put each other down in our society. How would Jesus want his followers to treat one another?

> *Lead a life worthy of your calling, for you have been called by God. Be humble and gentle. Be patient with each other, making allowances for each other's faults because of your love. Always keep yourselves united in the Holy Spirit, and bind yourselves together with peace.*
>
> (Ephesians 4:2–3)

Think about the ways in which men and women put each other down in our society. How would Jesus want his followers to treat each other?

How should you be treating the guys in your church, friendship group, family or school?

Chapter Ten
Girl of Gold

Refresh

In the hot Samaritan sun, the woman scuttled to the well to collect water. Head down, keen to avoid the crowds, desperate to hide away from the comments and criticisms that surrounded her on a daily basis.

'Apparently she's been seeing another man.'

'Really? What happened to the last one?'

'I don't know, but she obviously isn't much of a keeper. And all those children with different dads. It's a crying shame.'

'She should be ashamed of herself!'

'She'd better collect water in her own time. I don't want to rub shoulders with the likes of her. Just imagine if she had her sights set on our husbands . . . '

It had gone on for years: the taunts, the mutterings of disapproval, the exclusion. Her life wasn't conventional to say the least, but things weren't what everyone thought. She didn't mean to move on from one guy to the next, but when you are poor and abandoned and have a habit of easily falling for the wrong man . . .

She sighed as she reached the edge of the well. Someone was already there, and it was a man. This was all she needed – more fuel for the gossips. He looked like a foreigner as well. 'Well at least he won't know who I am,' she muttered to herself. 'If I just keep my head down perhaps he'll ignore me.'

But he didn't.

'Can I have a drink of water, please?' he asked her in his thick northern accent.

She looked up at him, amused and bewildered. Everything inside her wanted to scream at him, 'Why are you talking to me? Don't you know who I am and what this looks like to people in this town? They treat me as if everything I touch is somehow tainted. Or do you know all this and want to add to my bad day?'

Out loud she asked, 'Why do you ask me for a drink?'

Jesus looked down into the water in the well. Then he turned to the woman and began to speak the words that were to change her life for ever.

'If you knew who it was who was asking you for a drink, you would be asking *me* for water. The water that I could give you to drink is not like this stuff in the well. In this heat you'll soon be thirsty again, and you'll have to keep coming back here for more.'

'Yeah, and face the judgmental crowds. I don't know how much more I can take,' she thought.

'The water I could give you would change your life from the inside out,' continued Jesus. 'I know all about your life. The different men, and the fact that the guy you are with is not your husband . . . '

'How does he know this about me? How does he know that every day I have an ache inside, a thirst that nothing and no one can satisfy? Who is he?'

'The water I could give you to drink would come up from inside you – you won't need to collect it from a well. You will always have it in you, quenching the thirst in your heart and soul.'

Moments later, the woman left her water jar and the foreigner at the well and ran into town, banging on all the doors, yelling excitedly at people, 'Come and see this guy I met at the well – he knows everything about me! He's knows how I tick and who I am! Come on, you can get this life-changing water from him too!'

What a transformation. In one meeting with Jesus she discovered a love and a hope she thought she had lost. From that moment on, everything changed for her.

What does Jesus want to help you discover about yourself?

Are you prepared for all that you are yet to discover?

Secret Riches

Imagine that your reliable source got in touch with you again and told you that there is a never-ending supply of diamonds hidden in rocks under the ground. Based on what you discovered last time you acted on her advice, you decide to make it your life's mission to find them. After attending a crash course on how to dig for diamonds, you get your gear together (hard hat, light and pick) and head for the nearest mine.

You arrive at the entrance to the mine and take a deep breath. It's going to be hard work and you don't know exactly where the diamonds are hidden. You are going to have to trust your instincts and keep working away at the rock face until you find what you are looking for.

You get down on hands and knees and crawl down the mine to the rock face, where you start chipping away at the rock with your pick.

Hours, days, weeks and years go by.

You chip away at the rock, bit by bit.

Some days you see a tiny diamond sparkling brilliantly against the black of the rock. Other days you don't find anything at all. A couple of times you hit a diamond seam and find more diamonds than you know what to do with.

But, whatever each day brings, you are determined to keep on picking away at the rock, certain that there is more to find. When you have gone for days without finding any diamonds, you convince yourself to keep going. When your hands are sore from all the work and your back feels that it is breaking you take a few deep breaths and remind yourself that there are more diamonds to find – and you keep going.

Whatever the mine throws at you, you just keep going, because you know that there are more diamonds to uncover.

At the beginning of this book I asked you what you were striving for. I suppose I was wondering what you are digging for – what are you pouring your energies into uncovering?

Some girls want fame. Others want popularity or wealth. Now you know that you are chosen and cherished by the Creator of the universe, what are you going to do with the life he has given you?

There are so many different ways to live life; you can feel excited, anxious or even scared.

Here is a list that a group of 16-year-old girls have come up with about how their attitude to life has changed over the past few years:

'I know more about what I am looking for in life.'
'I feel I have more responsibility and am trusted by my family more.'
'I wear different-coloured tights and refuse to go along with the crowd!'
'I think more about sex, my sex drive and sexual pressures than I ever used to.'
'I know that when God says he forgives me he really does – and I can forgive myself.'
'I feel much more mature and much more aware of people around me than when I was younger.'
'I have become more of a young lady and want to be more honest.'
'I reckon I am more focused at school and am not going to be taken for a fool.'

'I look back and regret some things I did – but I know I am not that person any more.'

'I feel stronger bonds with old and new friends.'

'I am learning how to control my emotions and how to deal with the pressures of school and stuff at home.'

'I feel like I can take more risks in life but still think about it first.'

'I have grown into the real me and have learnt to respect myself and stop putting myself down, as I know from my friends' help that I am better than that.'

What an incredible list!

It goes to show just how much change happens to you in your teenage years.

Standing still isn't an option.

Burying your head in the sand and hiding away from the difficult things in life isn't the way to live.

The truth is that in your life you will face difficult times. Friends will let you down. You might not always succeed at everything you try. Someone you love might get ill. People close to you will die.

This is the way of life.

Knowing that God is always with us doesn't mean that we will avoid suffering or getting our hearts broken. He does promise, though, that in the middle of the darkest and hardest times in our lives we will uncover something beautiful about him and the life he has given us. His promise is that, even when we can't see or feel his presence, he will always be with us. Just like the diamonds in the rock, we know that God has more in store for us than we have already discovered.

This is the mystery of life.

What do you think your future will hold?

What are your dreams?

Take a moment to let your imagination paint pictures in your mind of your future. God will inspire you. He might give you a picture or a feeling or a bunch of words about what he is planning for you. Although he knows all about your life, he wants you to dream big with him.

> 'For I know the plans I have for you,' says the Lord. 'They are plans for good and not for disaster, to give you a future and a hope.'
>
> (Jeremiah 29:11)

The following prayer was written by a Christian guy over a thousand years ago. I love it because you can feel the passion the writer has for God and his commitment to be totally focused on God's plan for his life. Read over it a few times so that you understand what he is saying. If you want to, read it out loud as your commitment to listening to God about your relationships and future.

> Shall I abandon, O king of mysteries, the soft comforts of home?
> Shall I put myself wholly at the mercy of God?

Shall I leave the prints of my knees on the sandy beach?
O king of Heaven, shall I go, of my own choice, upon the sea?
O Christ, will you help me on the wild waves?
(St Brendan of Clonfert, c. 484–c. 577)

Thank you for coming on a journey with me through this book.

I hope that, when you make mistakes, you will be quick to admit where you went wrong and do what you can to put things right. I trust that when people let you down you will be slow to jump to conclusions and quick to listen. I hope you can learn to forgive people and see hope where everyone else sees despair. Could the woman written about at the end of the book of Proverbs become a role model for you?

She is clothed with strength and dignity, and she laughs with no fear for the future. When she speaks her words are wise, and kindness is the rule when she gives instructions.

(Proverbs 31:25–26)

But it's time to draw all this to a close. So let's end as we began.

You have been created in unique and wonderful ways by your Father God, who loves you.
You are precious and your life is a gift to you.
It's a secret because few of us know it and fewer actually believe it.
But now you know the secret.
Now is your time to choose to accept it.
Your present is waiting for you.
This present is yours, uniquely yours.

No one else can claim it.

But the weird thing is that you already have it.

It was given to you from the second you were conceived.

When you looked like a little tadpole in a pond,

When no-one else knew you existed.

When you were given your eye colour, height, personality traits, a way of laughing, a way of being you ... even before anyone knew you were there.

He knew you were there.

And he gave you a present: your identity, purpose, name.

And that name is

daughter.

Your name means cherished, loved, lovely, precious, you.

It means that your life is full of adventure, challenge, responsibility and possibility.

It means that, although you will know the best and the worst of times, you will never be alone.

It means that you will always be loved for who you are.

Let the truth of God's love live in you.

How are you going to live it out and share it?

How are you going to use your God-given loveliness and talents to transform your world?

The world is waiting for you, girl of gold. Now is your time to shine.

> *If you are filled with light, with no dark corners, then your whole life will be radiant, as though a floodlight were shining on you.*
>
> (Luke 11:36);

I will give you treasures hidden in the darkness – secret riches. I will do this so that you may know that I am the Lord your God, the one who calls you by name.

(Isaiah 45:3–4)

May God's words of wisdom continually pour into your life the kind of things that help you know that you are lovely, lovable, unique, full of potential and, above all, cherished.

Rachel x

Notes

Chapter 1 The Beginning of Mysteries
1. *One Tree Hill* is a US television drama for teenagers, directed by Mark Schwahn and first aired in September 2003 on the WB TV Network.

Chapter 2 Lovely label
1. *Jane Eyre* (BBC, 2007) (DVD, 2006); directed by Susanna White.
2. Charlotte Brontë, *Jane Eyre* (Smith, Elder & Co., 1847).

Chapter 3 Uggs in the Rain
1. Mother Teresa, *A Simple Path* (Ballantine Books, 1995).

Chapter 4 First-time Club
1. Anne Frank, *Anne Frank: The Diary of a Young Girl* (London: Valentine, Mitchell and New York: Doubleday, 1952).

Chapter 5 Holy Body
1. Nigel D. Pollock, *The Relationships Revolution* (IVP, 1998).

Chapter 7 Death to Bad Sex
1. *The Holiday* (Columbia Pictures Industries, Inc. and GH One LLC, 2006); directed by Nancy Meyers.
2. David Delvin, *The Good Sex Guide: The Illustrated Guide to Enhance Your Love-Making* (Carroll & Graf Publishers, 1993).

Chapter 8 What are You Waiting For?
1. *The Virgin Daughters*, a *Cutting Edge* documentary by Jane Treays about

the Purity Movement in the United States (Channel 4, 25 September 2008).

Chapter 9 Nice Guys

1. *Enchanted* (Walt Disney Pictures, 2007); directed by Kevin Lima.